CAPRI
AND
NO LONGER
CAPRI

Other Books by Raffaele La Capria

FICTION

IN ENGLISH

A Day of Impatience, translated by William Weaver, 1954

Mortal Wound, Farrar, Straus, 1964

IN ITALIAN

Amor and Psyche (Amore e psyche), 1973

Three Novels About One Day (Tre romanzi di una giornata), 1982

Japanese Flowers (Fiori giapponesi), 1979

Snow on Mt. Vesuvius (La neve del Vesuvio), 1988

ESSAYS

False Starts: Fragments for a Literary Biography (False partenze. Frammenti per una biografia letteraria), 1974–1995

Lost Harmony (L'armonia perduta), 1986

Literature and Somersaults (Letteratura e salti mortali), 1990

The Eye of Naples (L'occhio di Napoli), 1994

The Apprentice Writer (L'apprendista scrittore), 1996

The Fly in the Bottle: In Praise of Common Sense (La mosca nella bottiglia. Elogio del senso comune), 1996

OTHER WORKS

Feeling in Literature (Il sentimento della letteratura), Mondadori, 1996

Neapolitan Graffiti: How We Were (Napolitan graffiti: come eravamo), Rizzoli, 1998

The Unintentional Novel by R. La Capria (Il romanzo involontario di Raffaele La Capria), No editor. Liquori, 1996

Conversation with Raffaele La Capria (Conversazione con Raffaele La Capria, Navvare l'armonia perduta. 1995 Nuova Omicron Gaglianone, Paola

CAPRI AND NO LONGER CAPRI

RAFFAELE LA CAPRIA

TRANSLATED FROM THE ITALIAN
BY ELIZABETH A. PETROFF
AND
RICHARD J. PIOLI

THUNDER'S MOUTH PRESS / NATION BOOKS
NEW YORK

Published by
Thunder's Mouth Press/Nation Books
161 William St., 16th Floor
New York, NY 10038

Nation Books is a co-publishing venture of the Nation Institute and
Avalon Publishing Group Incorporated.

This book was originally published in Italy, in 1991, under the title *Capri e non più Capri*. Some of its chapters—specifically, "The Dream of an Imperial Villa," "The Discovery of the Blue Grotto," "Savinio's Capri," "Romantic Monika," "The Solitary House," and "On a Rock One Morning"—appeared in *Corriere della Sera*. "My House Under Monte Solaro" was published in *L'Espresso*.

Library of Congress Cataloging-in-Publication Data

La Capria, Raffaele, 1922–
   [Capri e non più Capri. English]
   Capri and no longer capri / Raffaele La Capria ; translated from the Italian by Elizabeth A. Petroff and Richard J. Pioli.
     p. cm.
   ISBN 1-56025-348-7
   1. Capri (Italy)—Description and travel. 2. La Capria, Raffaele, 1922— Journeys—Italy—Capri Island. I. Petroff, Elizabeth. II. Pioli, Richard J., 1953– III. Title.

DG975.C2 L313 2001
914.5'73—dc21

2001034711

9 8 7 6 5 4 3 2 1

Designed by

Printed in the United States of America
Distributed by Publishers Group West

CONTENTS

TRANSLATORS' PREFACE

In his charming book about Capri, Raffaele La Capria does not shrink from undertaking what he considers to be a most important obligation, the need to go through and beyond personal recollection to visualizing that island as one of Western culture's metaphors for its own dissolution and eventual disappearance. As personal memories incline toward the elegiac, so too can such a place as Capri evoke the sense of loss we all experience with time's passing and, on a deeper and broader level, our civilization's changes and its ceaseless exploitation of the natural world. This is a global phenomenon and each of us has his or her own Capri to treasure and to mourn, and chances are that in the childhood of each of us there are experiences that generate emotions similar to what La Capria feels about his magical island. We too were once Titans roaming a new and beautiful world all our own, unsuspecting of the changes we would undergo or see brought about in our surroundings. *Capri and No Longer Capri* evokes this feeling about the world in a more prosaic but no less emphatic manner than does Cesare Pavese in his *Dialogues with Leucò,* a beautiful account of the Greek childhood of our own culture, with its tragic vision and innocent gods and their eventual disappearance, once myth gave way to the rational explanation of human consciousness. It is to this profound conclusion—our loss is very real and very bitter—that La Capria turns in his final chapter; but there is much to explore before the reader gets there, especially if Capri is the armchair traveler's actual destination, if the reader is in fact standing on the quay of the Marina Grande, waiting to discover what it is Capri may have to offer in these late days, for it is truly we who are the ancient ones.

Americans have now been visiting Capri for many years and La Capria's book will offer newcomers to the island much they would not otherwise have at their disposal, for his book is a guidebook of a special kind, something like a novel *and* a local Italian guide, a cultivated cicerone, or perhaps a primer on how to align oneself with universal feelings; how to experience other people's feelings about such a beautiful place, its history, and those monuments both natural and human. Once a traveler has decided to pass more than a few hours here, then La Capria's quick succession of insights, memories, and reveries may become an essential key to gazing into the very heart of this beautiful place.

Without running through the usual chronology and list of sights, La Capria gives his reader the sensation of having peered beneath each stone, and of having reached an appreciation of what such a place has done to others, some of whom, once under Capri's spell, gave their lives over to their dreams. The traveler who reads *Capri and No Longer Capri* while visiting Capri has the great fortune of both imagining the place *and* experiencing it, which may well be an improvement on La

Capria's opinion that you cannot see the island without first imagining it. Instead, we are able to add our imaginings to his, and this may transmute a typical itinerary into its opposite, from a rushed and common aggravation into a preternatural sense of being at home. This tiny island, once the home of gods, then emperors, and currently home to Italians and Europeans, also calls to us in the New World.

Be sure to take this small book with you when you go to Capri, and by all means make sure you go. It is a very complex island, historically, culturally, presently; it would have to be so if Capri can represent the entire world in microcosm. For those American travelers accustomed to breezing through a European capital or province in a single day, Capri can be too easily overlooked, unappreciated, and perhaps misunderstood. It is not Saint-Tropez. When it is not simply checked off by travelers as having been done in a day, all the sights and sentiments that La Capria describes begin to emerge, as with the Aleph of Borges' story, "the place where all the places of the world meet without mingling, beheld from every possible angle at once."

In the Postscript to the Italian edition of this book La Capria wrote, "It is desire and not nostalgia that better explains how we are what we are, and how things have reached the point they have. And the desire to reencounter those places where our roots reach down also matters, in order to—even through writing—reappropriate them and 'make them feel at home in the world.'" What better way to express the native son's "personal geography" to those of us who seek the fulfillment of our desire. While many North Americans travel to Italy because they are of Italian descent, many others travel in order to learn, to confront another side of their desire, and Americans have often explained who they are in terms of such desire. To this purpose, La Capria assists them in carrying out their postmodern Grand Tour, which must inevitably draw some of its power from nostalgia, just as this book does. But it is a text that is by no means simply fixed upon the decay of things, although this is a powerful theme. The Sirens' song may no longer enchant anywhere on this earth, and still we generate new meaning and undergo other experiences and we find such adventuring personally desirable. So too with a trip of reasonable duration to Capri in whose course the person well attuned to seeking beyond the obvious maze of touristic promotions and entrapments still is able to wonder at extraordinary places, and is able to feel accompanying extraordinary feelings there. Literature combines with travel to make a mighty potion. One may choose not to agree with La Capria, who believes that "on Capri, as in all the loveliest places on earth, one can always best discern the impending threat of finality, of the 'world's disorder' that inevitably moves us to consider the decadence and the end of all things." If that were all there was to see, we would remain in North America in order to receive our lethal dose right here. Chances are that what we will take away from a visit to Capri will more closely resemble La Capria's love of the place, and the love that so many of the people he describes also had for it.

Capri has had a long history as a place of retreat, as one of sensual license, and of unparalleled natural beauty. Its immediate effect on the visitor is ambiguous—the menace of its looming cliffs, the warmth of its sea and sun—and in many of the stories La Capria tells about the island this same ambiguity recurs. He begins with imagining Capri as it might have been when the Roman emperor Tiberius took up residence there. Succeeding chapters are devoted to celebrated visitors from northern Europe and to the writers and literature associated with Capri. And everywhere he tells us about spots on Capri that can be sought out and visited. The long final chapter is La Capria's "journal," devoted to the landscape, the spirits that inhabit it, and the melancholy erosion of its beauty by modern life. But here he also alludes to the sense of the beautiful that he learned from Capri, to the state of grace he knew in the past and still feels now, in dialogue with the universe from the terrace of his home at the foot of Monte Solaro. Standing at one or another of Capri's many exceptional sights, the visitor will understand La Capria's philosophical state of grace, his ability to think in universal terms before unparalleled examples of natural beauty; for far removed from the piazzetta, with its teeming crowd of sightseers and cafes, remain the silent, secret, and perhaps still "sacred" sights: Monte Solaro, Villa Damecuta, Villa Jovis, the non-Catholic cemetery; the *Scala Fenice*, the Arco Naturale, the grotto of Matromania, the Certosa, and many others not usually reached by day-trippers, and all of them splendid occasions for taking La Capria out and reading him.

And once we have returned to our homes, within *Capri and No Longer Capri* we bring back much of that astonishing place and its extraordinary inhabitants, both literary and historical, to remain upon our bookshelves against the time it will be taken down and reopened, remembered, felt anew, and shared with others. In this way, we never leave Capri again: it is better to have seen it in order to go on imagining it and dreaming it.

ELIZABETH PETROFF AND RICHARD PIOLI
Capri, Summer 1998

CAPRI AND NO LONGER CAPRI

THE DREAM OF AN
IMPERIAL VILLA

"If you do not dream the world before you see it, then you cannot see it." It is the same with Capri: you cannot see it unless you have first dreamed it. Only in this way can it appear before you as the mythical place where Nature first encountered Beauty, as the purest image of the sea that was once the cradle of the gods, as that island from which Ulysses heard the Sirens' song. It was always that call that worked upon the northerners to create the myth. They were "the dreamers with flaxen hair" who discovered Capri, who revealed it to us. But it is only natural that it should have been thus. It is always the other's gaze that discovers and reveals us to ourselves. This relation with the world and things created by the Greeks and inherited by the Romans, which has always aroused nostalgia and inspired romantic attempts at recovery, here seems to have found a perfect place for imitation.

These unassailable heights, these peaks from which Tiberius "kept watch for the signals he had ordered to be sent from the mainland to inform him how things were going" (at the time of the conspiracy of Sejanus)—while he kept his ships ready for flight if it became necessary—these "cliffs bursting forth from out of the abyss," are full of history; they make us feel how ephemeral history is in comparison with the eternity of nature. And they both remind us and undo the interlacing of the many lives that came together here, attracted by a mysterious call. And so for me Capri often resembles a kind of observatory, some extreme limit, where it is possible to reside only after you have acquired the strength and resignation it takes to sustain the notion of the inevitable end of all things, even of Capri and its myth. Because the sharpest sensation of the world's coming to an end assails you in beautiful places like this. And here, suddenly, in the pale-azure calm of the day, you are startled by that silent moment in which "you face with a shudder the ineluctable fact that you too will die."

I was thinking about these things as I was reading Cesare De Seta's book *Capri* (ERI Publishers, Turin, 1983). But, having got almost to the end of his volume, I was struck by a most suggestive image, situated where I wouldn't have expected to find it, in the chapter entitled "Guide to Monuments." It is an image based upon a hypothesis that also forms a part of our dreams and helps us to see. The hypothesis is that Capri, during the Augustan-Tiberian epoch, may have been "a single, immense villa," connecting various nuclei of buildings meant for ceremonies, for habitation, and for service; and that in reality the "twelve villas" whose ruins have been discovered in various locations were only one. "Twelve imperial villas, even for a lovely island of varied beauty, are, in reality, a bit too much," wrote Maiuri. "We may talk at the most of *villae rusticae* and of *villae fructuariae* of the freedmen farmers and administrators of the *patrimonium principis*." But that Capri was completely imperial property, and that upon this property at least three large villas were inhabited by the emperor, appears to be accepted by everyone.

Islands transformed into villas were the fashion, especially along the coast of Campania. Was not Lucullus' villa the island of Megaride (where the Castel dell'Ovo stands today)? And were not the little islands of Gaiola and Nisida near Posillipo once Roman villas too? If Lucullus and Vedius Pollio were permitted the luxury of owning island villas, we can imagine that the combined magnificence of two emperors permitted the same thing to be done on a much grander scale on Capri, to build upon this special piece of property, now become a park, a mountain villa (Villa Jovis), a seaside villa (the Palatium, with the "Baths of Tiberius"), and a country villa (Villa Damecuta on Anacapri, at that time surrounded by a version of Arcadia). The great park for these three villas had belvederes, terraces, woods, gardens, exedras, and nymphaeums scattered about everywhere (at Matromania, at Castiglione, and Migliara). It had enormous cisterns for water, it had baths, pavilions, pools (the model of the enclosed pool, you can imagine, was the Blue Grotto!), and it had two private landings, one at the Marina Grande (beneath the Palatium) and the other at Tragara, in the reflecting water opposite the Faraglioni rocks. Doubtless these locations came together to form an organic whole. And, as Capri was always linked to that image of the imperial island-villa, so it was also located right in the center of the sea that the Romans used to call *nostrum* (look at any historical atlas to confirm it); from there Augustus and Tiberius ideally were able to scan their entire Empire, from Greece to the beaches of Africa and Spain, and, in order to set off for Rome at a moment's notice, were able to have the fleet, anchored at Capo Miseno, within easy reach. Beautiful and inaccessible, Capri was therefore the perfect refuge, adapted to every possibility, because its geological conformations guaranteed security and privacy; and to every season, because the various villas corresponded to different kinds of vacations. And so it was that later it became "the model for the Neronian villas at Subiaco and for the Domus Aurea itself, as well as for Domitian's villa at Castelgandolfo and for Hadrian's villa at Tivoli."

If this image of the fantastic villa with a park that occupied the entire island were really the truth, then it would well agree with the matter of one of the more unique chapters of this book, the chapter dedicated to water. Not to the (once upon a time!) stunning and transparent blue-green sea that surrounds Capri, but to the water of the rain, to the fresh water of the (very few) natural springs, "which was the disaster that united all the various islanders."

"The road to water for Capri," De Seta writes, "is comparable to the great roads to gold and oil that have plowed up the history of much larger territory." It was precisely the exceptional development of these imperial residences during Roman times that also led to a network of huge cisterns built at key locations. These cisterns determined the location and the form itself of each dwelling place, and it was the need for water that in a most original way determined the architecture of Capri's houses: "The relation between these enormous reservoirs and the small habitations that collected around them must have been in itself a peculiar trait of this countryside." ("The cisterns formed the center around which the entire complex of Villa Jovis was organized," writes Maiuri, "and with their branching canals they are like the heart of some organism with arteries for blood.") But De Seta extends this idea to encompass the entire island, and so it is as if water, the need for water, "had shaped in an indelible way the architectonic forms of the island itself: the unity and homogeneity that have always been recognized in Caprese architecture derive from this deep-seated reason." And is it not a curious coincidence that Tiberius' villa was dedicated to Jove, also known as Jupiter Pluvius, the god of rain?

Back then, to one catching sight of the great villa from the sea, it must have appeared more like a natural fortress, an (imperial) eagle's nest, rather than some magnificent abode of the fantastic type painted by Weichardt around 1900. Unscalable rocks and peaks, a shoreline for shipwrecks, beetling and merciless crags fit to discourage anyone—with good or evil intentions—who dared to approach the place. We can then understand Tiberius' anger when in an anecdote recounted by Suetonius a fisherman boldly did scale the cliff that loomed over the abyss and suddenly presented himself before the emperor with the gift of a mullet. Was the emperor's inviolability not safely assured? Could any assassin who carried a dagger instead of a mullet reach him? Tiberius ordered that the mullet be rubbed in the face of the poor boy, who, with a detachment and presence of spirit clearly of Parthenopean stamp, exclaimed as he suffered this cruel treatment, "Thank heaven I didn't bring a lobster!" Anyone else would have laughed. Not Tiberius. He ordered the boy's face torn to pieces with a lobster. And to think that Suetonius did not spend a single word in homage to this unknown hero, who perhaps climbed the horrendous cliff at the risk of breaking his neck to ask only some small recognition.

At that time, Tiberius must have been in his seventies, an embittered and spoiled old man. But who knows if all the instances of his iniquity and cruelty recounted by his chronicler are true? Even then the journalists who wrote of the lives of the powerful—for such was Suetonius—loved to slam the monster on page one as soon as death had rendered him harmless.

Caligula followed his uncle to Capri, and it is incontestable that he may have been the first to introduce extravagance, the real thing, and not only in his style of dress. From atop his rock-bound villa Tiberius had watched the starry heavens and the constellations of the clear summer nights, his astronomer Trasillus beside him, the only being who had the emperor's complete trust and who interpreted the signs and portents for him. In fact, Tiberius was quite superstitious and most respectful of his gods and those of others.

Legend tells us (and Tertullian confirms it) that Pilate, two years after having condemned Christ to death and returning by sea from Palestine upon completion of his commission, stopped to render the expected homage to the emperor. And where, if not on Capri, did Tiberius reside at the time? This was a custom, indeed an obligation that—and you can imagine how scrupulously—all the great dignitaries from the distant provinces of the Empire acquitted themselves of upon their reentry into the fatherland. Pilate had not been able to erase from his disturbed conscience his encounter with Jesus of Nazareth, Tertullian writes, and he even averred "that he had already become Christian in his soul." He then told the emperor the story of Christ the Galilean—whom no one in the West had ever heard of at that time—and of how he had been judged and then placed upon the cross, and of how he had returned to life and risen into heaven, according to what his followers say, turning back the great stone that had sealed his tomb. Tiberius must have listened to this tale with interest, even anxiety. Who if not a god would be able to rise from the dead? "And so Tiberius, at the time when the name of Christian made its entry into the world, submitted to the Senate the news that he had received from Palestine, which showed this divinity to be so widely known there, and he gave his own favorable opinion," Tertullian goes on to say. In other words, he sent a letter to the Senate in order to have Jesus accepted into Olympus and recognized by the gods. Whether or not this legend is true or, much more probably, merely opportunistic cannot be proven, but isn't it already quite an extraordinary stroke of luck that the name of Christ made its "appearance on this earth," and that means in the West, which means Rome, starting from a tiny and unreachable islet in the Mediterranean, named Capri, barely larger than a rock?

Even today as you approach the island from the sea you do not see much that is agreeable, no open shore to embrace warmly whoever comes along. The island's geological configuration is such that it looms everywhere and you begin to wonder, "Where are the homes, where do they live?" You see dwellings nowhere except for a narrow line of them as you enter the port of the Marina Grande. To tell the truth, Capri's beauty is the kind that must be discovered. Enclosed like a nut within its shell, it is like the gardens of the Alhambra, invisible from the outside and surrounded by walls that deny even a lucky guess as to what marvels are contained within. (Unfortunately, the tourist agencies always take it upon themselves to give them all away.) Both the island's disconcerting appearance and the "gossip-inspiring" presence of Tiberius necessarily gave rise to the many legends that survived until the change in romantic culture's attitude toward the spirit altered that image, and until those men from the north, whom I've already mentioned, revealed an absolutely different way (even literally) for the island to be seen.

In 1664, Daniello Bartoli described Capri as "an incoherent mess, either a building or a landslide (you cannot really tell) of monstrous stones, one atop the other, rising, climbing up, flying to the stars. And with such steep cliffs around every turn, the island has steep, demolished shoulders around which everything is grouped together, so that it might be called the Cliffs of the Hopeless: nowhere on Capri is there a cliff or a ridge that isn't at such an immeasurable height that if you leave it you're sure to crash or plunge yourself into the abyss of the deep sea that surrounds her. If Nature had tried to design a lonely and impossible place where all the vices of the whole world could be exiled, she couldn't have come up with anything better." It is said that the author had never seen Capri, just as he had never gone to China or Japan, even though he spoke so well about them. But the beauty of his language makes us forgive him for his unreliability.

Even the great Goethe, who passed Capri on his return voyage to Naples from Sicily, seemed to have been struck with the same superstitious fear. He saw "the rock above us, not offering even tiny inlets or indentations on which to place a sure step." He saw "the steep and ever more sinister cliffs . . . as a soft twilight still swept across the sea," and on one perfectly tranquil day—fearing that the ship, the wind having fallen altogther, was about to be driven onto the rocks by the current—upon considering their situation "with horror"—he invited the ladies aboard to "address a fervent prayer to the Madonna," and imagined that several Caprese shepherds he had glimpsed upon the mountain were shouting for joy at the prospect of an imminent shipwreck and the "rich booty" they would recover from it.

This is what is meant when it is said that someone has a good imagination!

And until the early years of the twentieth century, with Diefenbach, one had to resist the image of a spectral Capri that loomed forth out of a fog upon the sea like a sphinx of rock (as in one of his paintings). Who knows why the stubborn Danish painter insisted on representing the island as the setting for a

Poe story, despite all the stupendous and sunny mornings and the tender and rosy sunsets he must have seen so many times. But by then, ever since the time when Kopisch arrived there in 1826, the discovery of a Capri truly at the height of myth had begun.

Lucky was the person who knew the marine Eden, the portentous transparency of its waters, the inviolate silence of its morning, the happiness of being there upon some rock and thinking of nothing! This happiness certainly shines forth from the pages of Gregorovius, who stretched out upon the sand of the Marina Piccola one summer day in 1852: "Sitting there one can only believe in the world. The Bay of Naples, its shoreline, the islands, its sails have disappeared as if they never existed; one's sight wanders over the immensity of the sea, in the direction of Sicily and of more distant Africa. . . . Early in the morning, when the sea began to glimmer, I often heard the hoarse cries of the seabirds, as they swooped down from their rocks to fly above the waves. And during the evening, when everything was so peaceful, from atop the Faraglioni rocks their mournful cries could be heard. Who could listen to them and not be overcome by a feeling of melancholy? Their cries are sad like the harmonies of Aeolian harps, and they carry you back unintentionally to past desires . . . One could spend long hours here enjoying the sea breeze and considering the effect of the light upon the sea: everything is still, everything glistens; the waves and the rocks gleam in the heat of the morning, and at midday only the monotonous song of the cicadas can be heard. Light, air, fragrances, all things are in harmony; the soul becomes drunk with solitude."

Doubtless Capri's image has changed and continues to dye itself with ever brighter colors. It became "a rock issuing forth from the Tyrrhenian, with its marble mountains and small green valleys, with its cones and pyramids against the sky, its grottoes and caverns in the water, its gradations of violet and its incomparably sweet blue, with doves and seagulls accompanying each other through the air, as the rosebush and the sea fennel together issue forth from between the rocks, with the temples of the fallen gods and the palaces of the dead Caesars, with gardens enameled with flowers and populated by birds, and the gracious curves of an amphitheater populated by boats and circumscribed with nets, with its churches of Christ and of Mary allied with the altars of Mithras and of Jove, beneath garlands of pines and embroideries of foam, between the Bay of Naples and the Gulf of Salerno, with Vesuvius enflamed and the serene gulf before it, and the limitless sea behind it, festooned with capes and promontories of classical design, bearing ruins of religious sublimity, this Eden, in a word, that has no rivals in this world."

These lines by Castelar, a literary Spaniard who visited Capri in the 1870s, must have then been a description (a bit Art Nouveau perhaps) according to the taste of the time. But in its emphasis and in its "sublimity" one can already foresee the Capri of "divine earthlings" that was to explode shortly thereafter.

The style of Norman Douglas is dramatically different. A profound connoisseur of Capri, Douglas spent a great many of his years on Capri and died there in 1952. Although he was one of the last of the Victorian rebels to fall in love with the sun and Siren Land, he never lost his critical mind or his sense of humor:

"There are wondrous tints of earth, sky and sea in these regions—flaring sunsets and moons of melodramatic amplitude that roll upon the hill-tops or swim exultingly through the aether; amber-hued gorges where the shadows sleep through the glittering days of June, and the mad summer riot of vines careering in green frenzy over olives and elms and figs; there are tremulous violet flames hovering about the sun-scorched limestone, sea-mists that climb in wreathed stateliness among wet clefts, and the sulfurous gleams of a sirocco dawn when fishing boats hang like pallid spectres upon the sky-line: there are a thousand joys like these, but the natives do not see them, although, to please foreigners, they sometimes pretend to" (Norman Douglas, *Siren Land*, p. 98–99).

THE DISCOVERY OF
THE BLUE GROTTO

Whoever reads *The Discovery of the Blue Grotto on the Isle of Capri*, by August Kopisch, can only smile at the ingenuousness of the author, who was certainly a polite and gracious writer, but not much more. Stricken with the ardent love that so many romantics come down from the north had for our land—for its still intact beauties and for its people—August Kopisch arrived on Capri with his friend Ernest Fries one summer day in 1826. As we see him leap upon the "resounding sand" of the marvelous island and walk up to meet the "simple people, fishermen and gardeners . . . perfect reminiscences of the beautiful people of ancient Greece," our gaze follows him, slightly uneasy before his capacity for transfiguration.

Luckily for him, he stumbled upon the inn of the esteemed Notary Don Giuseppe Pagano, and the two became friends. They took walks together and visited the ruins of the villa of Tiberius; they climbed the steep stairway to Anacapri; they scaled Monte Solaro with Teutonic purposefulness. August

Kopisch, a poet, naturally was reading *The Odyssey* and, obviously, was imagining Odysseus as he sailed past the Sirens' rock and heard their song. He even managed to dream that on Capri in those golden days "her good youths engaged in wrestling and boxing, in racing and javelin throwing, and in all the graceful dances, according to Greek custom." Who knows how many of the island's mysteries recounted by his host, Don Pagano, concerned Tiberius and his iniquities? After all, on calm summer evenings the sweet white Capri wine, so sulfurous and tart, a pleasure going down, would flow. On one such evening the story emerged of a marvelous grotto, a grotto that everyone told stories about but that no one had ever beheld. The German was immediately attracted to the idea of discovering it.

In reality we know that, even back then, the fishermen of Capri were fully aware of the grotto, and as I read the pages that described its discovery the suspicion came to me that Don Pagano, the canon uncle, the boatman Angelo Ferraro, and the notary's young grandson as well—for the fun of it as well as to please Kopisch—agreed to make their enthusiastic foreigner believe that entering the mysterious grotto would be an extraordinary enterprise never before attempted. And just to make it seem still more extraordinary, they brought forth their entire repertory of superstitions, fables, and legends with which our tradition is so rich: the grotto was inhabited by the devil and by evil spirits, and by sea creatures, and so on. And one of the most surprising parts in Kopisch's little book, which indeed does not omit many surprises, is the account, delivered by the canon to Kopisch, of a Triton that had been harpooned by a fisherman.

"How did that happen? A fisherman had gone down to the vicinity of the diabolical grotto in order to fish with his harpoon. That morning was so splendid that he could see the conch shells creeping along the sea bottom, as deep as sixty fathoms.

Suddenly he saw all the fishes dart away except for one that remained upon the bottom. It began to advance higher and higher and circled the boat. Because the fish was as long as a man, the fisherman held the sturdiest of his harpoons in his right hand, tightly tied the rope, and stood waiting in ambush with the oar in his left hand. The fish kept rising. It gleamed red, then green. Even its eyes were flashing red and green. The fisherman had never seen such a fish and became strangely worried. But, instead of reciting an Our Father like a good Christian to make the fish descend, he screwed up his courage, as the saying goes, and as the fish got closer to him he launched his harpoon in the name of the devil. He saw it penetrate the neck of the fish, but the sea grew so red with blood that soon he was no longer able to distinguish anything. He believed that he had killed it with that one blow, since the rope had gone slack, and immediately he began to pull. But wait a minute! Up came the harpoon without the fish and without its fork, in two pieces, not broken but as if it had melted. Then he was really scared! He dropped the harpoon in the boat, took up the oars, and started rowing with all the strength he could muster. But the boat, instead of pulling away from that spot, spun around in a circle just as the fish had done earlier. Finally everything stopped, and out of the red water there emerged a bleeding man, with the fork lodged in his chest, who threatened the fisherman with his fist. Then the poor fisherman fainted and his boat was pushed by the waves all the way back to the Marina. He awoke to find himself being aided by his friends. For three days he remained silent about the whole affair. Finally, on the fourth day he was able to tell what had happened. But then something extraordinary happened to him. The hand with which he had thrown the harpoon began to dry up and wither like a leaf. Little by little all his remaining members withered away in the same manner. Finally his body and his head were both so wrinkled up that he had to die. His body did not have the appearance of a corpse but looked more like a dried root in an herbalist's shop."

Doesn't this story sound as though it came from a fantasy written by Alberto Savinio? This tale and others like it—"Greek fables"—the Capresi told the German, perhaps to make his sojourn upon the island more interesting and in order to make the mysterious grotto more fascinating to discover. And even if, as I have supposed, they were putting on a comedy, there is no doubt that as they were telling these fables to their foreign guest they were energized by his emotion.

And so one morning in that summer of 1826 the adventure began. How beautiful Capri must have been that morning, in the grandiose solitude of Mother Nature! And if instead of an adventure it was only a comedy, every one of its actors knew how to deliver the required drama during the performance. Most of all Don Pagano, in the role of one who at the last moment, standing at the grotto's entrance and gripped with fear, wanted to call the whole thing off. Finally the "discoverer" swam through the rock's narrow crevice, but having blinded himself with the smoke from the torches in a tub that he was pushing ahead of him, he was unable to see anything. Then "in terror" he noticed that the water beneath him was "like the light of a blue flame," which is a fine image, for that really is the color of the light that emanates from the water of the grotto. He seemed to be swimming "in an unfathomable blue sky," and a tingling ecstasy made him tremble before that "marvel of the world," before its "magnificent and unparalleled colors," and he shouted to his fellow adventure-seekers to come in and share his intoxication. But the others, once they were inside and not terribly excited, probably because they had already seen the show, went on with their comedy and came out with the idea that there was also "Tiberius' corridor" to investigate, and told the story of a tunnel excavated in the rock that connected the grotto to the Villa Damecuta, the Roman villa standing directly above the grotto. Kopisch, who "did not find the thing improbable," scrambled onto a kind of landing, lit a candle, and, just able to make out a dark opening, entered it together with his friend Fries and the other members of the expedition. Something from the fables he had heard must have remained in his head, because his imagination was so excited that he mistook a stalactite for a specter; so afraid was he of his own shadow that he looked "not back but only to his side," and fancied he was being assaulted by God knows what. Then he discovered "a window," a perfectly square opening that bore the trace of human handiwork and that can still be seen today, an evident sign that for some sacred or profane reason the grotto truly had been frequented by the Romans. All this exploring distracted Kopisch somewhat from "that wavy sky" beneath him, which emitted such a magical light. But how could a romantic voyager of that epoch, and a German to boot, return from such a place without his dear portfolio of sketches from life? "We swam outside in order to get our field chairs and our satchels . . . then we sat ourselves down at the window . . . and thus we carried to conclusion two views of the grotto." These were the first views of the endless series of Blue Grottoes—more blue than any other, blue below and blue above and blue along each curve of its vault—that spread to every corner of the earth, causing this marvelous grotto to undergo the strange destiny of all places overrepresented: it was erased and transformed into a non-place by the excess of representations.

While Kopisch and his friend sketched, the others swam and bathed "like black devils in that splendid water," and "wherever the waves crashed, there sparkled azure." However, in the middle of that exaltation "Don Pagano, for whom our sketching went on a bit too long, left us. He had business in Capri and he couldn't remain as long as he would have wished." Which shows not only the clear practical sense of Don Pagano (and of every good Caprese) but also that our suspicion that the whole of it was a comedy is not unfounded after all. "Even the most beautiful of days cannot last forever," Don Pagano seemed to be saying, "and business is business."

Reference must also be made to the intervention of the proprietor of the land above the grotto, a man who, out of the exasperated sense of ownership that obsesses every Caprese, believed in good faith that the Blue Grotto belonged to him, that it was his thing. He too went in to have a look about and, having bumped into some stones that appeared to be remnants of masonry, he threw himself upon them and cried out, "There's a treasure here, and it's mine!" Which drew laughter from the others.

With the sketches finished, there was a final exploration of the grotto and the passageway, where Kopisch got lost, like Pollicino in the fable, before finding his way again. Eventually he reached open air but only with the firm intention of further investigating the marvels he had just seen.

In order to get back to the Marina Grande, the discoverers made some kind of circumnavigation of the island, and the most relevant part of Kopisch's description is where he writes about the Faraglioni rocks and their shore: "Until now no artistic reproduction has been known, perhaps because the waves, which are always so high right there, are an impediment to their being drawn." Those were the days! Unfortunately, in the next century the seas quieted down and the Faraglioni raged in paintings, photos, and postcards, with success and excess equal only to those of the Blue Grotto. But the story of Kopisch's discovery does not end there, because like a good German he did not consider the job finished until he had explained the phenomenon that produced such a magical effect of light. One day when the calm sea allowed, he went down to the marina and rowed back to the grotto. This time he entered during the afternoon, the best time, and after many conjectures he came to the obvious conclusion that the grotto's light is caused by the refraction of the sun's rays as they pass through some underwater opening. These "scientific" conclusions seemed to satisfy his Teutonic exactitude and he returned to Don Pagano "quite pleased with the happy outcome of his second visit to the grotto."

There was the final visit, made in the company of "the young and daring Prince T. and the Count of L." Here, because the seas were rough, one speaks of "audacity" and of "temerity" upon the moment of entering, but when the three find themselves swimming in the grotto—and "the breakers beat like an immense blue flame whose foam seemed like smoke as it dispersed" and "was dissolved in a rain of blue fire upon the roaring water of the interior, such that the waves seemed to become a million trembling gems"—the description rises, it seems to me, to the height of the occasion. But not even before this grand spectacle does our poet's Teutonic pedantry give ground, and after a short time, as his two companions (who, I don't know why, have all the airs of two chic somebodies) enjoy splashing about in that marvelous water, he is occupied with taking the measurements of the grotto: "a bit more than one hundred feet in length and somewhat less in width, and half as deep. The height of the vault spanning the water . . . was estimated to be more than thirty feet at its greatest."

By then the enterprise could be said to be complete. Everything was seen, explained, measured, every mystery unveiled, and the Blue Grotto—so it was baptized by Kopisch—was ready to be relinquished to future visitors. "For me," wrote its discoverer, "it was enough to describe something that I truly saw and lived."

Is it possible today, as you enter the Blue Grotto, to still feel some of that emotion that assailed its first discoverer? I wanted to try the experiment. One afternoon I took a boat and went there when the hours for tourist visits to the grotto were almost over for the day. I had not returned in years. Before the entrance, beneath the gaze of the little Madonna who keeps vigil above that pagan place from her niche in the overhanging rock, was a throng of boats loaded with tourists awaiting their turns. One boat sported a sign advertising "Tickets 7000 lire per person." A cashier-boatman was collecting entrance fees and boatmen-guides were scrambling to pay. Smaller, narrow boats were rapidly loaded with four or five tourists apiece, lifted out of the larger boats; an uninterrupted stream of them was continuously entering and emerging from the grotto's narrow opening amid screams, exclamations, and cries from the visitors. There were Swedes, Japanese, French, people of every race, but all identical at that moment, each with his or her hat of straw or of cloth, predominantly elderly, patient in the sun, and a bit disoriented from having to realize in such a hasty and unpoetic world the dream that had seemed so beautiful in the tourist brochure. This rite, which unfolded before my eyes, recalled another that took place during the war when there were houses of prostitution with lines of waiting soldiers and students, payments to a cashier in return for a ticket (or stamp), and the moment when a vague but desperate amorous desire was transformed into a hasty encounter with an impertinent harlot.

I was about to leave, when the last boats, visiting having ended, went off in a procession with their load of upset tourists. I remained alone before the grotto. I entered and, after a few seconds, I saw the blue. It rose from the bottom's blue porthole like a luminous exhalation, dispelling the darkness of the earlier impression, and the black rock all around seemed suspended above the magical light that defined the surroundings so sharply. I had been admitted into the most secret part of the island, where its blue heart lay beating. I dived into that blue. As I swam, my legs enflamed it, as embers catch fire beneath ashes, and with each movement the blue, opaline on the surface, blazed sparkling forth, and innumerable furrows marked the water, superimposing blue upon blue. I too was *"hanté,"*, as the poet says, by the Blue! Blue! Blue! Blue!

Can it really be true, as Norman Douglas writes, that "no one, none of us, thinks of returning a second time to the Blue Grotto"? I tried it and I believe that I will repeat the experiment.

FERSEN: A LEGEND IN SOMEWHAT BLACK AND PINK

For Capri the discovery of the Blue Grotto signaled the beginning of its prosperity. Norman Douglas wrote that the Blue Grotto "has created hotels, steam-boats, and driving-roads; it has stuffed the pockets of the gentle islanders with gold, transforming shoeless and hatless goatherds into high-collared Parisian cavaliers; it has altered their characters and faces, given them comfortable homes and a wondrous fine opinion of themselves. Long live the Blue Grotto! It has lately built the funicular railway; it has dappled the island with the villas of eccentric strangers."

To be honest, these eccentric foreigners didn't come to Capri just to see the Blue Grotto. There were plenty of other attractions that drew them to these parts, and the greatest one of all was a kind of felicity that only the Mediterranean could offer.

I want to dream of being on an island in the South
with a beautiful shining sea before me,

immersed in golden air.
I want to dream of lying upon a rock,
watching the sky hollowed out by the light
and me there dreaming . . . beneath the palms.

This dream that Heine's verse invokes is dreamed sooner or later by every northerner. It was a dream that, to be realized, very much required a backdrop of sea and sun along with a constant undercurrent of eroticism.

The cult of the sun was one of the most surprising revolutions in the modern history of feeling. In the nineteenth century the "poetic" celestial body par excellence was the moon; in the twentieth century it became the sun (Paul Fussell, *All'estero* [Bologna: Il Mulino, 1988]), and among its adepts figure the great immoralist writers of the twentieth century: from Gide, Lawrence, Douglas, Huxley, and Forster to Isherwood, Auden, Spender, and others. While, until the end of the century, people of quality had preferred to distinguish themselves by their pallor—and to be pale signified being romantics, and the whiteness of the female body attracted concupiscence and profane desire—by the first decade of the new century the bronze-skinned "walked nobly among those with paler skin like sovereigns among their courtiers."

Forming part, if not the dominant part, of the undercurrent of eroticism was something that Jean-Jacques Bouchard, with a finesse completely French, alluded to as *"la courtoisie,"* when he came to Italy in 1632. "The ladies are very beautiful and so are the young boys," he wrote, "and both gladly perform the courtesy." And Roger Peyrefitte, in his now famous *L'esule di Capri,* explains with great enthusiasm and wit what this courtesy was like:

That of the boys is complete, because they perform it indifferently in confronting both sexes. Capri or Taormina, all Italy is hermaphroditic and this is the secret of its exceptional beauty.

A miracle that I attribute, like all others, to Catholicism, sees to it that this particular courtesy does not in any way alter the virtues of the race. The entire world steps upon the Italians as if upon marble. They dance their tarantella for us. They are ready to dance it naked, as you may have noticed at Sant' Angelo, and then they go off to join a religious procession. Our menservants, whom, let's face it, we cause to be seen in every light, leave our houses as white as snow. They have, or soon will have, their girlfriends and will want to get married in order to have babies as soon as possible. The first models of Gloeden and Allers are now the good fathers of families, after having given joy to their masters. Within the deepest grottoes of Capri, the Grand Duke of Hesse and his associates are working, unknowingly, to create homes and hearths. Through mysterious channels, so much misspent love ends up within the breasts of mothers.

And so many foreigners, Germans most of all, and then the English, the Americans, the Swedes, and the French, began to arrive on Capri, attracted to our celebrated "courtesy."

It is true that at that time in Italy there was a curious incoherence between the availability of boys for "courtesy" and the severity of the laws that punished it; between the broadness of views in the families of those boys—who considered it great luck to entrust a young boy to a rich, eccentric, foreign gentle-man—and the narrow views of the public opinion that objected to these agreements. And quite aware of it were Fersen, Allers, and Douglas himself, all of whom were constrained many times to leave the island suddenly until such time as the waters disturbed by their exploits had calmed down. But those in love with the Mediterranean were not discouraged and the cult of the sun mingled in their imaginations with the cult of young boys, and the Greekness of the sea with that of love. The availability that they discovered to be agreeable (especially in the south) made them into enthusiasts for the country, and they became inclined to abandon themselves to their deeper, hidden desires. These youths and small boys shrank before nothing and their naturalness, their spontaneity, and their readiness were truly pagan; even miraculous, if one considers how greatly unattractive those eccentric gentlemen were. And so the sun, the ephebes, a spot of decadent aestheticism, and a dash of real Nietzscheanism combined to form an irresistible brew for whoever felt called. And out of this also perhaps came the conviction that the people of the south were less hypocritical than those from the rigid, puritan countries of the north, and that the sun was the cause of this "precious sincerity," an altogether northern notion that was bitterly contradicted by the facts some time ago, when that event took place that came to be known as "The Krupp Affair."

But it must be said in all honesty that Krupp did not come to Italy with those intentions. Even though they were attributed to him, I am inclined to believe that he never sought or received any "courtesy." Whether he unconsciously desired it, no one can say. However, when he arrived in Capri in 1898 and took up lodgings in the Hotel Quisisana, it was simply because his doctor had prescribed it for him. He suffered from attacks of asthma, depression, and circulatory disturbance, and the Capri air, he had been told, would do him good. It could not have been too good for him, since four years later he committed suicide.

Even Norman Douglas did not come to Italy with those intentions; rather he had married a cousin and had a house in Posillipo, on Gaiola. But then "his vision of the Mediterranean as the natural frame for the seduction of very young people" took root and guided him for the rest of his life, until, too old and sick to continue, he committed suicide at eighty-four.

Fersen committed suicide at the age of forty-four, the paternal warnings of Douglas himself notwithstanding, who in *Looking Back* relates the following colloquy that took place between Count Adelsward Jacques Fersen and him.

Fersen had offered Douglas a pinch of cocaine, which he accepted.

"I didn't know you took snow."

"I don't make a rule of it."

"Pouf!" Fersen said. "I do."

"So I perceive. Do you want me to tell you, Jacques, what a damned fool you are?"

"You told me that long ago, when I used to smoke opium."

"Do you know what you are doing to yourself now?"

"Nobody knows it better. I have nothing left to live for save—this. My life has been messed up."

"It is you who are messing it up. . . ."

"Messed up by other people. You know?"

"I know. Send them to Hell. Don't go there yourself."

"Ah, *mon vieux*, if I had met you when I was a boy!"

This conversation took place when Fersen's parabola was reaching its end point. He had come to Italy the same year that Krupp killed himself. In Rome he met Nino Cesarini, a fifteen-year-old boy, the son of a news vendor on the Via Veneto. They returned together to Capri and the following year took possession of the Villa Lysis, which Fersen had built near the ruins of the imperial palace of Tiberius, and there, in an atmosphere of decadence in the manner of a Des Esseintes—saturated with an oppressive, sickening narcissism and with ceremonies, opium, rituals, and myths—they nourished that black and rosy legend in which they were both the protagonists and the victims. The story is famous and has been told more times than it deserves.

As a poet, Count Adelsward Fersen was not too refined, ending up becoming quite maudlin:

> *I will be your slave with sweet submissive eyes,*
> *filled with love and melancholy for you.*

Et cetera. You immediately understand the type and its argument, how it will end as well. Douglas found him to be theatrical: "He had the Neronian taste for self-exhibition," he writes, "his speech was easy but superficial. Vanity had rendered his head emptier than was appropriate; some lovable traits, some touches of genuine sensibility appeared from time to time," and Douglas remembers "his youthful freshness, his blue eyes, his clear complexion and perfect build," also observing that he was overly precise in his dress, or too well hung. In her book, *Capri, frammenti postumi*, Lea Vergine writes that "according to witnesses, when Nino and Fersen went out in public, down to the Piazza, they revealed themselves like two Adonises, one dark and carnal, the other blond and diaphanous. . . . Fersen imposed the same white suit upon his 'valet,' and the same Panama hat, and even the coquetry of a malacca cane."

* * *

To give a clearer understanding of what type of fellow Fersen was, one of the many morbid and aestheticizing extravagances did cost him dear and forced him to leave Capri suddenly. It began when Fersen had heard from his friend Clavel about a stone, found in Capri and preserved in the Naples Museum, that recorded the sacrifice of Hypatus, a boy slave of Tiberius, who was sacrificed to Mithras, the sun god.

> *Gods, inhabitants of Hades, welcome*
> *me, more unfortunate than any other.*
> *I was not kidnapped by the Fates,*
> *but an unjust destiny imposed on me*
> *a violent and unexpected end.*
> *I had just reached the favors*
> *of Caesar, and alas! I no longer shall see*
> *the light. Hypatus is my name.*

It is striking, and even moving, to read this. But you can only imagine how much more striking and moving the mere idea of this barely adolescent youth stripped and sacrificed in such a cruel manner was for Fersen. All Fersen's sadomaso-homoerotic fantasies must have been stirred, and if you add some opium, the odor of which never left him, and his decadent taste for ritual, we arrive at the event that on Capri came to be known as "The Deed in the Grotto."

Fersen decided to "reenact" ritually the whole atrocious episode, to make it live again symbolically, with allusions to his relationship with Nino (allusions about which I know nothing and am not overly preoccupied with finding out). The fact remains that Fersen was dressed as Caesar, in gold sandals, toga, and all the rest, and Nino was dressed as Hypatus. And they were accompanied by a little cortege of crazies in Roman costumes. Men and women with Cingalese servants carrying torches approached during the night along the footpath that led toward the grotto of sacrifice, the grotto of Matromania near the Natural Arch. This place was wrongly believed by Fersen to have been a place dedicated to the cult of the god, because its name echoed Mithras-Magnus and also because Roman remains had been discovered there.

As the sun came up—for that was the sacrificial hour—Nino was stripped naked. While those present sang the verses to sacred hymns written by Fersen himself and the smoke from the incense curled around them, their Caesar raised high the dagger (a fruit knife!) and struck down into Hypatus-Nino, thereby producing a slight scratch that began to bleed somewhat.

The whole rite had been observed from some distance by a young country girl who was grazing her goats at sunrise. She told her family what she had seen. The family ran to the priest, and the priest ran to the local police, and in no time the matter grew to seem gigantic. Nino's nudity and Fersen's reputation immediately led them to imagine orgies, bacchanals, and what accompanied them. Fersen finally had to leave Capri in furious haste and he set off for the East in order to distract his attention. He returned to Capri after the scandal had died down.

Fersen died in 1923, having ingested an amount of opium far stronger than what he knew his body would tolerate. Why did he do this? Was it a kind of *tedium vitae* or for the sake of his narcissistic consistency? Compton Mackenzie captured quite well the fatuous side of his personality in *Vestal Fire* and yet there was also the tragic side that Douglas saw, despite the fact that he also considered Fersen to be a superficial person.

I end with a small detail that very indirectly connects Fersen with my own memories. Fersen's sister, Germaine, married the Marquis of Bugnano and lived with him in the Palazzo

Donn'Anna, where the Marquis kept a beautiful apartment with a view of the sea. During the thirties, when I was around ten, I also lived in an apartment in the Palazzo Donn'Anna, which I have often described in my books.

Krupp, Fersen, and Douglas. Three different and excellent suicides. Aren't they a bit too much? But Capri was the Island of the Sirens and those who heard their song suffered the consequences in various ways. It has been written that "their soothing voices bewitched the sailors by promising knowledge of all things." I think they were bewitched by the promise of happiness, with the union between life and the light of this place. In fact, the bones of those sailors seduced by that song are still whitening, calcifying, and they are mingling with the rocks of the Sirens.

KRUPP: AN ODIOUS CONSPIRACY

As soon as Krupp had arrived on Capri, he felt like another man; his ills (asthma and depression) disappeared and he rediscovered his serenity. He liked the nature on the island, the people of humble conditions who served him with the grace that all true Capresi can demonstrate to whoever in their judgment deserves it. He felt happy, he who had never felt so before. His father, a terrible and annoying *padre padrone* with an invasive, possessive, and authoritarian character, had always oppressed him, right up until the day of his death. He even demanded that his son, when still a small boy, take notes in a notebook while he was speaking, and recite back all the interesting things that he had said! When his father died he had to take over the running of the steelworks, or, rather, the "Krupp empire," and in meeting the challenge he had displayed ability and wit and was continuing to do so; but the obligations, the responsibilities, the meetings, had begun to weigh upon him. Even the family routine became intolerable for him, with its receptions, salon conversations, the dinners organized by his wife, Margarethe, for their illustrious guests. A tremendous bore. Maybe this was why he had become the victim of depression and, to escape from it all, came here to Capri, far from his wife, his two daughters, and every other possible responsibility, and his stays on the island were for longer and longer periods.

This reserved man, who looked like a professor or a corporate manager, in the morning would roll up his shirtsleeves, step into a small fishing boat, and head out to sea. People even saw him rowing standing up like a fisherman, plying his oars in time with the other boatmen. He wished he were one of them. He always hoped that he would not be noticed, that people wouldn't recognize him and would take him for a tourist or for one of the many penniless artists who wandered the island. Most of all he fled the company of those foreigners from his own social class who on Capri formed a small colony of snobs, and this attitude of his naturally paved the way for the earliest gossip: why did Krupp always spend his time with people of humble condition, the boatmen, barbers, and servants?

Professor Behring, the discoverer of the anti-diphtheria serum, lived at the Marina Piccola. Realizing Krupp's lifelong wish, he introduced him to the biologist Anton Dohrn, the director of the zoological station in Naples. Krupp was at last able to satisfy his old passion for study and research in marine biology. His happiness was complete. It was the first time that he succeeded in doing what seemed unimaginable to him. He had brought from Kiel his forty-ton yacht *Maja*, suitably outfitted for deep-sea fishing, and the next year, enthusiastic after his first successes (which had led him to the discovery of nine marine species, for which he gained recognition), he brought with him another yacht, much larger than the first, *The Puritan*, 350 tons, which seemed like a ship and left the Capresi in open-mouthed admiration the day she arrived.

Krupp lived at the Hotel Quisisana, owned by one Signor Serena, an ex-waiter who had made a fortune and who in the Communal Council was of the party opposed to that of Signori Pagano and Morgano, the proprietors of the Hotel Pagano and the Cafe Hiddi-gei-gei. Krupp did not frequent either of these places, perhaps in order to avoid meeting fellow Germans, but this fact naturally induced jealousy, resentment, and even ill will, deeply felt if unavowed. Not only was Krupp constantly generous to the islanders, handing out gratuities whenever it occurred to him, which amazed them, but, with a view to providing work for the poor during a time of serious unemployment, he gave an enormous sum of money to build what would later become the Via Krupp, which still stands today, proving, as Roberto Pane has written, "that even a road can be a work of art; and not just in a manner of speaking but truly in the aesthetic sense of the word." This is clear to anyone who, gazing down from the belvedere overhanging it, can see past that road's present state of abandonment. Krupp also donated to the Commune of Capri the land upon which rose the Gardens of Augustus, all of it with the exception of one lot, purchased from him by Michele Vuotto, an astute farmer from that area. Certainly Krupp would never have let it go to him if he could have foreseen that one of Vuotto's sons, in defiance of every law, would erect upon that most beautiful site the Hotel Luna, which by its huge size would disrupt the harmonious connection between the Certosa and the Gardens of Augustus and completely spoil the noble atmosphere of the location.

In the spring of 1902, the Via Krupp was completed and on the second of April the appreciative citizens of Capri conferred honorary citizenship upon Krupp. But his new happy life was to be quite short. A mere four years had passed since his arrival at Capri, and who would have thought that in the autumn of that same year this idyll between Krupp and Capri would end in tragedy?

While Krupp was in Germany the Communal Council was engaged in the election of the mayor of Capri. The political battle there is no less ruthless than it is in Rome, and perhaps can be even more so, because in a small place hatred is more readily cultivated and becomes more exasperated, and also because on an island when private affairs enter the picture, their input, proportionately speaking, is enormous. In this sense Capri has often reminded me of ancient Greek city-states, politically so quarrelsome, according to Thucydides' description of them.

Up to that time, the mayoral responsibilities were held by Serena, proprietor of the Hotel Quisisana and a good friend of Krupp. The party that wished to unseat him was led by Manfredi Pagano and Giuseppe Morgano. Serena won, but he won because he had spread a treacherous—and unauthorized—rumor; to wit, that if those supporting Pagano and Morgano in the Popular Party should defeat him, Krupp would never again set foot on Capri. This did not go down too well with Serena's adversaries, who decided to avenge themselves. They accomplished this through the mediation of a personage from the outside: the schoolteacher Ferdinando Gamboni, who had reasons for resenting Krupp because Krupp preferred to receive his Italian lessons from the other *maestro* on the island, Luigi Messanelli, who in exchange accepted a lavish salary. Devoured by envy—"the southern vice par excellence"—Gamboni sent an anonymous letter to the newspaper *La Propaganda* in Naples, accusing Krupp—as Douglas writes—"of those things that he, Gamboni, knew only too well." This local schoolteacher had in fact been sacked from his former job at the elementary school in Massa Lubrense for immoral conduct with the children and, to avoid the consequences of his actions, had had to emigrate to America, where he had lived by his wits for several years. But no one knew about this at the time of the scandal, or any such accuser would have been easily silenced.

There is no better way to give you a sense of this base intrigue than by quoting a few lines from that letter written by Maestro Gamboni (anonymously, its claims never proven) and which *La Propaganda* printed on the fifteenth of that October:

"What has been going on for years at Capri surpasses even the power of the Biblical description of Sodom and Gomorrah. On this enchanted isle, under the auspices of a rich sexual degenerate, there has emerged a circle of degenerates who have lived and continue to live by standing upon the shoulders of the rich gentleman. The stories that reach us are truly frightful: the most terrible pages of Kraft-Ebbing could not describe all that is happening on Capri . . . So many tramps have become rich standing upon the shoulders of this pig who pays with one-thousand-lire notes . . . We order the authorities in Naples to intervene and eliminate this hand of corruption, to throw the filthy personages in this even filthier drama into prison or an asylum . . . We are waiting for the Halls of Justice to expose this association for the obscene," and so on.

A few days later the same newspaper published another article that likened Krupp's lasciviousness to that of Tiberius, and it demagogically concluded in the same characteristically intimidating style: "O mighty workers of Germany who produce the riches for Signor Krupp, here is how and where the diurnal exploitation of your work is realized."

In October of 1902, Krupp was forty-four years old, although he appeared more like sixty (so Douglas thought when he first met him). If you look at one of the photographs from that time you would not imagine that this middle-aged man, his gaze averted behind his gold-rimmed glasses and with the mild and bland air of a slightly paunchy family man, would have been capable of doing what he had been accused of and about which William Manchester writes, not verifying but taking these accounts at face value in his history of the Krupp family, *The Arms of Krupp*:

> A grotto was transformed into a terraced, scented Sodom. Favored youths were enlisted in a kind of Krupp fun club . . . they submitted to sophisticated caresses from him while three violinists played . . . orgasm was celebrated by skyrockets, and now and then, when the boys were intoxicated by wine and Krupp by his passion, the love play was photographed. [p. 231]

The same things that a tourist guide might say with an aim to scandalize are taken up and repeated in detail by James Money in his book *Capri: Island of Pleasure*. In reality, the aforementioned transformed grotto is the grotto of Fra' Felice, to be found along the sixth bend in the Via Krupp, where the road's namesake created a spot for innocent outdoor luncheons and of which photographs do exist and leave no doubt as to this much. Those other, scandalous and compromising photographs have never turned up, although they would have been most valuable if they had ever been uncovered.

According to what Norman Douglas writes in *Looking Back*, what Edwin Cerio writes in *Aria di Capri*, and what, recently, Carlo Knight writes in his well-documented and accurate work, *Krupp a Capri*, there was no truth whatever in all this slanderous gossip, only a matter of petty meddling treacherously performed by ignoble people. And yet—and even Douglas asks—why didn't Krupp react? He could have crushed his accusers; he could have hired the most prestigious lawyers on the Neapolitan Bar; with his money he could have bribed just about anyone if he had wanted to. Instead he did nothing. Was it from surprise? Was he bewildered by the betrayal? Was it from fear of dishonor or out of respectability? Or was it out of a bad conscience? Nobody knows; and so the accusations in *La Propaganda* were picked up in Rome by *Avanti!* and they inevitably arrived in Germany. On the fifteenth of November, the Socialist newspaper *Vorwärts* announced that "the richest man in Germany indulged in homosexual practices with the young boys of Capri."

The laws against homosexuality in Germany were quite severe and whoever ran afoul of them spent long years at forced labor. This did not prevent homosexuality from being quite widespread, so much so that sodomy was defined as "the German vice." And, Manchester writes, "the most virile men in the empire wrote gushing passionate letters to one another. Among the skilled practitioners of oral and anal sex were three counts, all aides-de-camp of the Kaiser; the Kaiserin's private secretary; the court chamberlain; and the All-Highest's closest personal friend, Prince Phillip zu Eulemburg und Hertefeld, who was sleeping with General Count Kuno von Moltke, the military commandant of Berlin. The King of Württemberg was in love with a mechanic, the King of Bavaria with a coachman, and the Archduke Ludwig Victor—brother of Austro-Hungary's Emperor Franz Josef—with a Viennese masseur who knew him by the endearing nickname Luzi-Wusi . . . During one party on the estate of Prince Maximilian Egon zu Fürstenberg, General Count Dietrich von Hülsen-Haeseler, the chief of the Reich's military cabinet, appeared in front of the Kaiser dressed in a pink ballet skirt and rose wreath. The general's ramrod back dipped low in a swanlike bow; then he whirled away in a graceful dance as the assembled officer corps sighed passionately in admiration. Hülsen-Haeseler circled the floor, returned to the imperial presence for his farewell bow, and then, to William's horror, dropped dead of a heart attack. Rigor mortis had set in before his brother officers realized it would be improper to bury him in the skirt. They had a terrible time stuffing the stiff corpse into a dress uniform" (Manchester, *The Arms of Krupp*, p. 230).

This was German high society at that time, providing the best subjects of research for Freud and Jung and nascent psychoanalysis. And yet, Article 107 of the German penal code was always a threat for whoever violated it.

After the article was published in *Vorwärts*, Krupp finally responded and had all copies of the newspaper sequestered. But it was too late and the Krupp Affair became a political case; it became a polemical weapon in the campaign conducted by the Socialists against the government and a means of propaganda against "the hateful warmonger Capitalism."

Events became further complicated after some good soul wrote Krupp's wife, Margarethe, an anonymous letter in keeping with the style of this entire edifying event, accompanied by all the Italian newspaper clippings referring to the matter. Margarethe ran to the emperor with the clippings; she had a nervous breakdown before his very eyes as she implored him to intervene. The whole affair was judged to be inconvenient, and most of all counterproductive, by all of Krupp's friends. At that time the only remedy they suggested, with Teutonic brutality, was for Margarethe to be institutionalized in a clinic, passing her off as crazy. Krupp complied, but the event unfolded before his eyes in a most dramatic way as Margarethe had to be taken away forcibly. No one knows what took place in Krupp's mind during the seven days that separated him from his death, on the twenty-second of November. Perhaps he repented of his conduct and of the treatment he reserved for his wife. He must have known to what degree he had been merciless with her and what consequences this would shortly have for his daughters. It is certain that he had her released immediately from the psychiatric hospital where they had taken her against her will. "On his last evening alive he dined with [their daughters]"—and it couldn't have been a very happy dinner—"then played *Salta*, a new parlor game, with them. Retiring early, he explained that he felt unwell. Outside, a dark bank of cloud hung low over the castle. By morning the sky had cleared . . . but Fritz did not see it. Precisely how and when he committed suicide will never be known; all that can be said with certainty is that the official accounts were so riddled with discrepancies that they were obviously a fabric of hastily constructed lies" (Manchester p. 236).

In *Looking Back* Norman Douglas writes, "I am aware that the legend of Krupp's aberrations has taken root, especially in Germany, where nothing about his Italian life was known and where it even led to the production of some literary trash (see page 319 of my *Capri*); my version, however, may be accepted as the correct one, not only because I knew him and his entourage and the entire population of the island, and would instantly have heard of such occurrences, but also, and chiefly, because I should not care tuppence if these insinuations had been true; I should think it rather sporting of the old gentleman to have indulged in love-affairs of any kind, at his time of life" (p. 157).

I believe Douglas' version because it seems so convincing to me. On an island like Capri, particularly in certain circles, one recognizes this kind of news; one always discovers the way to get at the truth, and Douglas was in a position to discover it. In the case of Krupp no proof, no witnesses, ever came to light. Therefore, when Douglas asserts that Krupp was not a suicide but in truth a murder victim, he is telling the truth.

Krupp is not a sympathetic personage. One who sells arms, who buys the patents and manufactures machine guns and long-range cannons (which were the cause of so many massacres during the First World War), one who, in order to save himself in extremis, has his wife committed to a mental institution, certainly is not sympathetic. Like many others of his stamp, perhaps he had a split personality; on one side a cold businessman, an able master of the foundry, and on the other, as Douglas writes, "also a German, in other words, a sentimentalist." And at Capri it was his second aspect that came out, among the simple people who felt that he was their friend. And then as his excuse there is also his oppressive education, received since childhood from a terrifying father who perhaps was the reason for any latent homosexual tendency in the son. Still, regardless of what it was, one thing is certain: an injustice had been committed against him.

And so it was written in *Il Mattino*, on 28–29 November 1902 in Naples, after the inquest took place at Capri directed by Judge Collenza, envoy of the general prosecutor on Capri: "Krupp was the victim of an odious conspiracy, of an atrocious calumny, created, it seems, with iniquitous spirit for the sake of a local battle by a Caprese electoral faction which was the losing party in the recent administrative election and the most bitter enemy of the victorious party. The saddest proof of just how much blindness can be produced by the passions of the soul even in a citizenry as gentle and civil as that of the main town on this enchanted isle, which seems thrown there, into our bay, by the great, vivid dream of a poet!"

And because, as the saying goes, "slander, slander, something will always stick," something stuck to Krupp. This perhaps is an even greater injustice.

DOUGLAS THE SIRENOLOGIST

The frequency with which the name of Norman Douglas arises every time one talks about Capri is a just recognition of his function as tutelary deity of the island. In him there is no trace of that exhibitionist narcissism or morbid snobbery to be found in so many of the other personages who played a part in the Caprese myth, with its string of names and the accompanying logorrhea. Of Douglas, John Davenport writes, "Rather than softening him, the sun of the Mediterranean mostly hardened him. The snows of Nordic puritanism melted but only in order to reveal the granite underneath."

With his book *The Story of San Michele*, Axel Munthe made more publicity for Capri than any other author before him, and it is certain that the second "incentive for tourism" after the Blue Grotto is owed to this huge work that is part autobiographical and part oleographical. However, while Munthe has now become an antique curiosity, a bit of kitsch like his villa in Anacapri, the fame of Norman Douglas is instead alive and thriving and shows no sign of diminishing. It is a fame owed to his work and to his style of living, the style of an ancient Greek, notwithstanding his many peccadilloes. "The only respectable event of my life," he said of himself, "was my birth. The rest is unpublishable." And it is quite true what Benito Iezzi writes: that "as in the island's consciousness Capri was Edwin Cerio, so Capri was Norman Douglas in international opinion."

In 1896, Douglas arrived in Naples. He bought a house on the islet of Gaiola at Posillipo and lived there with his wife for several years. Then they separated and a new phase in his life began, the so-called Greek phase that he pursued with arrogant independence for the rest of his life. From 1904 on, Douglas chose Capri as the place for his body and his soul.

His most famous books are *Siren Land* (1911), *Old Calabria* (1915), and *South Wind* (1917). Still, in traces and parts of *Looking Back* (1933) and *Late Harvest* (1945) you can feel the power of the lion's claws. In reality the great spring of Douglas stopped flowing during the First World War and never returned as before for the rest of his life. The loss must have weighed heavily upon him, if still in 1939 he could write to Cerio, "I am suffering from an ugly attack of graphophobia which threatens to become chronic. Do you know any cure?" Another illness that threatened to become chronic was his lack of money and of a decent place to live. He who had bought and sold homes and had discovered the most beautiful places on the island for building them—at La Petrara below the grotto of Il Castiglione, or at Caterola, for example—clearly was not practical or cautious in these matters, unlike others who had grown rich; he, alas, had to live out his final years in homes put at his disposal by generous friends like Compton Mackenzie, Kenneth Macpherson, and Edwin Cerio.

Returning to his writings, *Old Calabria* can in my opinion be ranked alongside Gissing's *By the Ionian Sea* (1901) and Carlo Levi's *Christ Stopped at Eboli* (1945), which remains the greatest one of all for me. In *Old Calabria* that capacity for seizing upon a place and feeling its spirit (an ability Lawrence also had) and at the same time communicating the magic of discovery is most evident. *South Wind* is also considered to be a noteworthy book by many readers, and perhaps it is. Douglas himself was convinced, however, that "no authentic son of man works well in a novel," and this book is a novel, his first and only novel. Perhaps his characters have something less authentic about them, which is not the case in the many life portraits scattered throughout his other books on travel and reminiscences. For my part, I cannot understand how this novel, a bit sluggish and labored, written in a style then in vogue, the "conversational" novel (the style of Huxley), was thought by readers from that period to be "a substitute for a vacation." Nor can I understand why the young readers of 1917 in the trenches felt that this book was about revolt, "a call in favor of youth, the sun and of tolerance directed at nations preoccupied with a suicidal war." Surely back then Douglas became a "cult writer" for many of that generation, and he remained one.

His greatest book is his most poetic as well as being his first. *Siren Land*, a voyage to the land of the Sirens, to the Bay of Naples and its environs, was composed when, fortunately for him, that region and all Italy was, for all its incredible natural beauty, its cities, and its monuments, still a visitable country. Afterward, our country became something of a Roman amphora—to borrow a beautiful metaphor of his—that was lifted out of the sea and now requires a lovestruck and practiced eye to be able to distinguish, beneath the encrustation that renders it unrecognizable, the harmony and beauty of its ancient form. In a short time, not even this much will be possible any longer. There are pages in *Siren Land* that remain in your memory, like the passage in which Douglas lingers to analyze with a poetic pedantry the nature and form of the rocks near Crapolla, a small inlet between Positano and Nerano. Or when he evokes the magic of a starry night at sea, observed from a dory as the fishing lines are lowered and the silent calm envelops him. Or one foggy morning when nothing moves upon the air or the sea and the world seems dipped in still gray.

However, regarding this work I have a small marginal and personal question for Douglas. How is it possible for a Mediterranean like him to say such awful things about our *zuppa di pesce* and the fish that we put into it? Let's begin with the *guarracino* that Douglas describes as "a pitch-black marine monstrosity, one or two inches long, a mere blot, with an Old Red Sandstone profile and insufferable manners" (p. 167). But did he ever see these blots in the sea, distributed throughout the blue in tight formations, like musical notes in a score? Or when in the empty blue sea only the *guarracini* are there, motionless and black, and they seem to swim inside a precious Chinese glass vase tinted the same transparent blue, with monochromatic designs of stylized fishes above? Then the *guarracino* is sympathetic, a kind of street urchin in the water like the sparrow in the air, so sympathetic that the Neapolitans have dedicated to it a beautiful song that still celebrates it. Douglas mentions the scorpion fish, *scorfano*, whose "name is unquestionably onomatopoetic, to suggest the spitting-out of bones" (p. 167). Here as well I do not dare contradict him. The scorpion fish does have a lot of bones, but there is no rose without thorns; its meat has a striking flavor that ennobles every *zuppa di pesce* in which it takes part. But I do not find it so ugly or heavily armored; rather, for me it is a classic example of pleasing ugliness. The needlefish, *aguglia*, "all tail and proboscis; the very nightmare of a fish—as thin as a lead pencil." Come, come! The needlefish, always swimming at high tide just a few inches below the surface and moving with the supple grace of a ballerina, reflecting the sparkling sunlight upon their emerald skin? Finally, there is the *tòtero*, or *calamaro*, the squid that, according to Douglas, is some kind of "animated ink-bag of perverse leanings . . . whose india-rubber flesh might be useful for deluding hunger on desert islands, since, like American gum, you can chew it for months, but never get it down" (p. 168). But if you see that little ink-bag right after it is caught, there are such sparkles upon its skin, such alchemical beauty. Its tender flesh possesses a light, sweet flavor that is a true delight.

"The fact is, there is hardly a fish in the Mediterranean worth eating," Douglas writes. And "there is not a cod, turbot, or whiting, or salmon, or herring in the two thousand miles between Gibraltar and Jerusalem; or if there is, it is never caught"; however, fish do exist there with "heads like Burmese dragons but no bodies attached to them"; the Mediterranean's "lobsters have no claws; its oysters are bearded like pards"; and then there are the *palamide*, "which are exported in thousands to the epicures of Naples and whose flesh tastes like shoe-leather soaked in paraffin" (p. 168–69).

Another northerner, Johann Wolfgang von Goethe, did write about the delicately delicious fish that one eats right in Naples. He was able to enjoy, as I also enjoy, a *dentice*, a *spigola*, a *sarago*, an *orata*, a *pezzogna*, fish never mentioned by Douglas. Was it because their flavor was *too* delicate for that eater of herrings with their overpowering odor? As for the Mediterranean lobsters, their flavor is incomparably more refined, even if they have less robust claws than those fished out of northern waters.

But it is better not to say so, since today so few lobsters remain in the Mediterranean and those, heading for extinction, must not be disturbed.

Well, having unburdened myself of those thoughts, I may return to my subject, which, however, concludes on a sadder note. When I saw Norman Douglas at Capri with Elsa Morante and Alberto Moravia, he seemed to me a generally contented man, despite financial hardship and age. He had been made an honorary citizen of Capri; he lived in a villa lent to him by his friend Kenneth Macpherson. He had Hector with him, a young boy of ten whom other boys taunted with *"puttanella,"* little whore. Douglas was then respected by everyone. He came from England directly after the war had ended; he had applied to our Consulate and our consul had asked, "Do you wish to return to Italy to live?" Calmly, Douglas answered, "I wish to return to Italy to die."

A few years later, in 1949, Giangaspare Napoletano interviewed him: "I was compelled to live on credit for the remainder of my days, and Capri is the ideal place for doing it. At any rate, I always carry two capsules of luminal." He said this as a joke, but he must already have had some presentiment or made some decision. At eighty he was "tall and bony with silver hair and a healthy complexion; he had more the air of a retired tennis champion than that of a writer, gently aged among his papers." This is how Napoletano described him and how he also appeared to me.

The winter on Capri is trying. The island becomes a dark and hostile rock, battered by rain and wind. In the evening not a soul ventures out, and it is cold, a damp relentless cold because southern Italian houses simply have no heating and the problem has always been dealt with in a very inexact way. Especially back in the fifties. It must have been an even more trying season for an old man such as Douglas, then eighty-four, full of infirmities and rheumatism, alone, with no friends or family (only a son far away; his friends had left in the autumn). The house where he lived was on the Tuoro road, number 23, not terribly far but far enough for him, and there were also stairs to climb. He had a fine garden with flowers and trees, in a well-constructed ancient style. He had a domestic who looked after him and he was cared for by Doctor Moore, an Austrian woman. He had, in fact, been attacked by a terrible, tormenting strain of erysipelas, or Saint Anthony's fire, which disfigured his face and caused him great suffering. As this disease worsened, his patience wore ever thinner and he grew "tired of being so mistreated," and it was perhaps then he decided to take his own life. The disease is derived from streptococcus and it makes the skin so red that it wrinkles and swells, causing a painful itch, pain similar to that from a boil, constantly stinging and throbbing. When it attacks the face, as in Douglas' case, it is even more intolerable, being so unaesthetic and repugnant to other people. It could not have been easy to live alone in the winter on Capri, with the rain, with the *tramontana* blowing, in a house one reached after something of a climb. And the winter of 1952 was an exceptionally cold one.

There is nothing terribly surprising about Douglas' decision. He did say that when confronted by a temptation, his response was always, "Why not, my dear man?" And so before this last temptation he would have said to himself, "Why not?" And then downed his luminal with the stoicism of an ancient.

THE CERIO-CAPRI
BINOMIAL

I sometimes ask myself if those travelers on their Grand Tour, who came to Naples and "discovered" us, contributed through their impressions and points of view to determining the split that allowed us to see ourselves as if we were passing strangers, and contributed as well to the preference for that excessive self-consciousness; the "performance," which is today one of the most obvious aspects of Neapolitan culture from the period of its decadence (as I have described it in *L'armonia perduta*).

Something similar must have happened to the Capresi, for there is no doubt that once they had been discovered and described by foreigners visiting from the end of the last century, their consciousness changed along with their opinions of themselves, and they developed a particular kind of rhetoric while remaining deeply connected to their insular culture, a *retorica caprese* that superimposed itself upon their concrete and practical natures.

But Caprese rhetoric does not belong only to the Capresi, nor is it simply a cultural construct. It is something more ambiguous, like an emanation of the place, and anyone can be influenced by it. I myself am not immune to it. For example, each time I set foot upon this island, I am filled for an instant by an inner exaltation, perhaps a more contemporary version of the Sirens' song. Then, it is true, that frisson passes, and the words used to describe it often end up sounding like mere rhetoric. It is not easy to come by words as nimble as Alberto Savinio's or a language as musical as Douglas'. But the rhetoric I have in mind is born of a feeling that really exists, and maybe this has helped to reinforce the Mediterranean myth that northerners have brought with them when they have disembarked here. The Capresi express this feeling in various ways, but most of all through the cult they have made of this island's history.

And so there is the dealer in rare, unobtainable volumes, the waiter who displays a dedication written by Graham Greene, or Neruda, or Roger Peyrefitte, in a book bestowed by the author; there is the owner of a grocery who collects curios; the telephone worker who owns a collection of old photographs and postcards of Capri from another age; there is the fellow who cuts out every newspaper article about Capri and has a true and proper archive in his home; another one devotes himself to the study of the demographic changes on Capri from the nineteenth century to the present day; and there is the person who opened a bookstore, La Conchiglia, and who now publishes an elegant *Caprese Almanac* that features in each issue the best writing about Capri from Suetonius on. Many of these islanders knew personally and have memories of Douglas, Malaparte, Moravia; there is also a friend of James Joyce. Joyce was never really on Capri and he does not play a role in its mythology, but how can he who wrote the modern *Odyssey* possibly have been a total stranger to the island of the Sirens? The islander Ettore Settani took care to establish a connection, never mind how indirect: with James Joyce (whom he met in Paris) he made an Italian translation of "Anna Livia Plurabelle," which they published in Curzio Malaparte's review *Prospettive* in 1940. Another admittedly indirect link with the culture that at one time felt thoroughly at home here and now must be inveigled into coming with lies and flattery has been established by one Graziella Lonardi. A Caprese by choice, she has transmuted the Malaparte Literary Prize into a sumptuous September feast, in which in recent years many notables have participated, among them Saul Bellow, Nadine Gordimer, Manuel Puig, Le Carré, Havel, and the Chinese writer Zhang-Je. And recently there has also been the Capri Prize, which Brodsky came to collect last year.

I think that if I were to ask these Capresi, who nourish this cult of Capri, the name of the writer they most prefer, the one who in their eyes best represents the myth that Capri has become in their imaginations and in their rhetoric, they would choose Ignazio's son, Edwin Cerio, most of all a writer but also an architect, a botanist, a naval engineer, a zoologist, and a paleontologist. Cerio the architect built the Casa Solitaria and such other villas as the Rosario and the Casa Romita. He is famous as a botanist for his *Flora privata di Capri*, an original and lively description of his involvement with plants; and as a writer he is best known for his *Aria di Capri*, in two volumes, one about its people and the other about its things. In these Cerio sought to create a Caprese mythology within a historical study of its particularly famous places, accomplishments, and personages. Writing about Axel Munthe and about theatrical mystification in his book, Cerio states that "one cannot explain Munthe with literary criticism. That takes island criticism," the only kind capable of handling the protagonist of Munthe's *The*

Story of San Michele and of demonstrating how unreliable he really is.

The same thing in a contrary—that is, a positive—sense can be said of Edwin Cerio: you cannot explain him with literary criticism. Island criticism is needed; it exalts Cerio because it recognizes his sincerity and his deep and true understanding of Capri. The island critic discovers that, among all those writing about Capri, he is the most pleasurable. A writer with his grace and his irony succeeds best in touching the feelings and fantasies of his readers, and if he exaggerates occasionally, the islanders understand and appreciate such exaggerations. For his part, the literary critic finds that heterogeneous cultural influences in Cerio are superimposed on or composed out of various and many contributions, verismo, futurism, decadence, "Mediterranean *Scapigliatura*," for example, without Cerio's ever succeeding in synthesizing them in an original manner.

The Capresi love Cerio most of all because they share his "rhetoric." It is this that often guides him: Capri as his vision of the world, his metaphysics, a personal obsession transformed into a vocational infirmity. It becomes a limitation, restricting his capacity to judge within terms that are as narrow as they are fanciful and digressive in the heavens of poetry: "All the great minds of Europe come to Capri for the stamp in their passport whereby they may enter into history, where the supreme activity of humanity resides: poetry, beauty, and art." It is also where Edwin Cerio happens to live, for whom some small sense of proportion would be highly beneficial. The theme of Capri as center of the world, as the boundary of absolute comparison and the measure of all things, appears in each of his books; it becomes insistent, a fixation. And if it is true that the artist is like an owl that always hoots the same verse—as Alberto Moravia would say—I also think that repetition enables him to refine it. But

Cerio becomes overbearing as he repeats it; he becomes rhetorical. So, two tones can be discerned in reading him, and the first of the two is rhetoric: "Capri, island of shipwrecks, azure melancholic, championship of humanity, rails of death upon which great derailed lives turn up ... Whoever clings to this rock-islet in desperation is saved by hope; whoever comes seeking Nothing discovers 'Everything' . . ." and so on, with capitalized words.

The other tone is the following and it is the one I prefer: "The southern, Neapolitan springtime, announced by the aerial bombardment of a storm, a flash of lightning, barely discernible at midday, and then a distant and sinister rumble. Across the countryside they say the thunder is needed to awaken the snakes that are still numb. Suddenly it is Spring. Eruptions of heat from the Sirocco inflame the morning sky little by little until it glows red with the golden heat at noon. And afterward comes the cool and soft breath of the northwest wind, the *Maestro*."

But the style that is most characteristic of Cerio is a pleasant, conversational style reinforced by a strong sense of humor, by his irony and propensity for paradox; everything that hits its mark when it doesn't become too insistent. He has a winning style, like a conversation you would not mind having continue, anecdotal, replete with observations, gossip, mischievous allusions, erudition. Pitigrilli (Cerio in disguise) inadvertently describes that style in a letter in which he asks Cerio to collaborate with him: "Dear Cerio, write me a short story with lots of color, very elegant, lots of strangers, and love, and snobs, very Edwin Cerio. But no philosophy, no poetry, no Soooooooul" (from *Edouini Caprensis*, edited by R. Bordone and D. Giorgi and published on Capri by La Conchiglia, 1990).

As he sketches the most characteristic personages of the island, at times he resembles Marotta and at others Guareschi;

and yet he is forever a born mythmaker. Even when he dons the
habit of a myth-undoer and wishes to "remove the mask
imposed by a decrepit notoriety" upon his island, he usually
ends up mythologizing. In sum, he produces a transfiguration of
facts and people, always attempting to surpass them, here with
irony and there with sarcasm, and over there with sublimation.
He always has something to do with "heroes," "masks,"
"myths," "shades," "demigods." Among his heroes he also
counts island people of humble circumstances, like the famous
stonemason, Maestro Arcangelo, a builder of "spiteful walls"
that were erected purposely to block a neighbor's view, and a
builder also of beautiful homes that, in these days, "appear
totally confused, appalled by the ugliness of the new houses rising everywhere around them." Here Cerio achieves the perfect
tone: "They say that Maestro Arcangelo built with his hands.
They really mean that he did not do things the way they should
have been done . . . the plaster, which he left rough, recorded his
fingerprints and is so uneven that the sun shining down plays
with the shadows upon the walls and makes them look like living things. In essence, he modeled houses and shaped them by
hand. He couldn't be called a genuine stonemason: he was an
artist first of all, he sculpted houses."

Cerio's humor and criticism are irresistible as he ridicules
Axel Munthe, who, in order to defend the poor quail and chase
them off the island, fired a cannon throughout the night—an old
cannon abandoned by the English in 1808 near his villa—and
sent the Capresi into a fury. As one knows, they are relentless
quail hunters and they waited impatiently for the arrival of
every May and September. But when Cerio writes his hagiogra-
phy of Krupp, he slips into rhetoric and misses his mark; he
transforms Krupp into a saint who "restored the well-being of
the workers, consoled widows, took in orphans," and then he

adds that "it isn't surprising that the Socialists murdered him; what is surprising is how long they waited before they did it." And here as well: "He sinned in having loved humble people too much, those who are poor, the disinherited: he was killed by the proletariat. The rabble never forgives." Right here I would like to say to him, "You know the rabble quite well, the names of the accusers are known, two Capresi not in the least bit proletarian; you know the name of the executioner, a certain *sorrentino* schoolteacher and the writer of anonymous letters, a stalker of children. But on the other hand, who has ever heard of a saint who manufactured machine guns and cannons?"

And yet that was how Cerio was built: he was temperamental, impulsive, generous, to the point of seeing things. So much temperament that he took plants to heart as well; his aversion to the bougainvillea is notable, a "lowlife plant" that was ruining the Mediterranean integrity of the Caprese flora with its exoticism and by cunningly taking root and proliferating undeservedly: "it is infesting every garden, corrupting even the outdoors, the innocent countryside, spreading its exotic poison of the worst kind of taste even into farmhouses. We must denounce the methods of this 'parvenu' that is close to claiming Mediterranean citizenship."

Finally, Cerio's battle in defense of the countryside and the natural beauty of Capri was sacred. This was expressed by him after he became the mayor and organized a "Convention on Landscape" in which the great names in Italian culture, from Croce to DiGiacomo, Ojetti, Murolo, Marinetti, participated. The *Convegno sul paesaggio* "solemnly consecrated before the rest of Italy and all other nations . . . Capri's right to protect its landscape patrimony." That was in 1923, when Capri was still—at least from this distance now—a marine and terrestrial paradise. Good thing Cerio never saw what came later! He intuited, with a sensibility made more acute by the beauty of the place (and by his snobbery), the environmental, ecological, and social disaster that is now under way. Prophetically, he warned us and he follows in the wake of all other prophets who wrote about this disaster, like Douglas and Lawrence, and for us, Levi and Pasolini. All these writers felt the end of a particular kind of civilization and the enormous consequences it would have upon the world's appearance and upon this country in particular. There is a part of Cerio that I feel very close to: it is his absurd reverie that "Beauty will save the world," now reviled by almost everyone. This reverie is not the mere dream of aesthetes like Ruskin or of "reactionaries" like Dostoyevsky, because now there are scientists who have begun to have it. In his *Fundamentals of Environmental Ethics*, Professor Hargrove discounts the necessity of preserving the environment for utilitarian ends. He insists we need to preserve it for aesthetic ends.

ALBERTO SAVINIO'S CAPRI

Ialways believed that Capri was an impossible subject, a subject that writers and artists would do well to avoid, because there is something so strong and overwhelming about the nature of this islet, something bewitching, that it renders every pretense of capturing its magic ridiculously inadequate. But reading the pages about Capri that Alberto Savinio wrote in 1926, pages luckily rediscovered in among his personal papers, has made me believe again. How intoxicating is the book that came out of them! How resplendent with "tingling flashes" his style, what a "diversity of light" illuminating each line, and how his words and images compete with the colors of the island to the point of reaching the same unrepeatable transparency! Surely, among the seventy-two short pages of Alberto Savinio's *Capri* (Adelphi, Milan, 1988), "a mysterious wind travels, a feathery guest, clever . . . and moves everything in a cool craze." Is this little quote not already enough to give you an idea of the unparalleled felicity of this writing? No one else has succeeded in re-creating with the enchantment of words the enchantment of the island within the soul of the reader. But miraculously Savinio has done it. And no one among "Ulysses' rowers—who, attracted by the never-ending song of the Sirens, have converged here from the remotest places on the globe"—has known how to imitate that song as Savinio has.

Only the most beautiful pages of *Siren Land* can compare with these pages, only those where sometimes Douglas seems to capture the cosmic vibration that sighs upon the air in Capri. But *South Wind* seems weighed down with a surplus of erudite and pedantic digressions and by a typically English and consistently ironic voice. And what of other writers? Compton Mackenzie seems a bit too worldly, Axel Munthe too improbable, Edwin Cerio too insular, Peyrefitte too romantic. They are therefore inadequate, to a greater or lesser extent, those other writers who describe daily life on Capri, "that idle, flirting life, sprinkled with hybrid crumbs of sentimentality, with middle-European aestheticism or with the cult of nature."

In 1928 and two years after Savinio, Filippo Tommaso Marinetti tried to describe Capri in his own way. What great times on the island back then! Marinetti wrote his eulogy for "Capri Capricciosa" and called the island "L'Indisciplinata," with "her galloping rocks" and "her hundred cliffs and jagged peaks" like "formidable and dynamic futurist architecture"(!); like "exclusive balconies for elegant suicides." He was so overcome with fascination for the island that he tried to imitate it in words: "Now I am swimming like a paintbrush in the blueblue between long glimpses of water." In that *blueblue* he discerns "intricate duels between reflections and sunrays" as he dives like a he-man into the turquoise water. "I part the blue madonna. I scatter the electric blue." But Marinetti's verbal bravado, even if carried out well ("long glimpses of water"), is followed by too much vulgarity: "You are a geological joke," he says to Capri. Even more directly he writes, "The insurrection of your rocks resembles the hygienic Fascist insurrection" (!!).

None of this emphatic stuff, none of this bravado, none of these extremely frequent lapses in tone do we find in Savinio's small golden book, written at almost the same time. In this work, hyperbole and artifice (that is, wherever they can be found) possess an incomparable lightness, more poetic than spectacular: musical, airy, taming. At times it seems as if one could see the words whirling between their lines like champagne bubbles.

"But is it really we who go to meet the island, or is the island coming toward us, having broken away from her granite anchors?" Savinio's voyage begins in the approach toward the enchanted isle, and he musters all the "proven science of the voyager" in order to describe it. Aboard ship he gazes at Vesuvius and he whispers, "O great mountain! More beautiful, and gentler, and sweeter than so many others I have seen. Remain a maternal, peaceful mother hen, the protectress of this entire sea and of her cities. Where was Leopardi's mind when he called you a 'formidable mount' and 'Vesuvius the exterminator'?" And after he half-prays like that to his protective god, his Mediterranean gaze embraces the gulf at the foot of the volcano, amid little coos of admiration from "all the Hyperboreans, and the Scythians, and the Barbarians, who invaded the south with a burning desire to become classicized," who are to be found aboard ship alongside him. Savinio has no need to become classicized himself, because he can hear the gods' voices, he has understood Circe, the ringleted goddess who counsels him and instructs him on his voyage through Siren Land (just as "the gray-eyed goddess" Pallas Athena aided Ulysses, the "hero of endurance"). And in fact Savinio tells us that he wants to remember that here is his true origin: "as soon as I set foot upon this island where each of us remembers being born, not in a real birth but in a metaphysical one."

Then his discoveries begin. He sees the boats at Marina Grande "lying upon the shore, resting upon their sides like seals suckling their young." He sees the little piazza in Capri, "that gentle, airy, flowery terrace that the inhabitants of these beaches built for centuries and centuries," in memory of dead Pompei. He sees the houses of Capri and the "evenly white, distanced columns, upon which rest a pergola's white rafters." He sees "the tomato face" of Spadaro, "decorative fisherman," who looks as though he were "born old," and who is "to Capri what Wagner is to Bayreuth." He walks the streets of Capri, that are "so narrow that two people must turn sideways to pass each other, like the reapers of King Hyksos," and where "the local and country life mix strangely with the hermetic and the international." He enters the labyrinth of its streets, "all closed-in narrow little pathways and corners, steeped in its smells and its labors." He sees "this island that inside a basket of granite gathers everything most colorful and fragrant that southern flora has to offer" and he also sees the rocks of Capri as they "carefully gather upon their peaks the last rays of the sun, and rise then at vespers as grave, still, tragedians illumined by the low lamps of the limelight." He travels down every lane of Capri in his wandering, "abulic, no resistance, blunders . . . temperamental streets, like Magyar violinists" (what a delicious companion to Savinio's style is his irony). And then he comes to the Faraglioni rocks: "There they are, way down there, natural and not painted, those famous Gothic cathedrals with their spires and their ramparts rising fiercely out of the sea. The water swells and sprays about, emerald in the shadows, a shimmering lamé where the sun beats down. In the decor of the Faraglioni, the surrounding sea is of great importance." And he observes this sea from the height of the "spinning, deceiving, totally pagan, panorama of Capri" and he sees its surface, "passing like a sail, like moving crystal upon the mysteries of the deep, where, between the dark banks of algae and the black mouths of abysses, phosphorus fragments of moonlight watch with the eyes of the medusa." He feels "the deep silence except for the tender rustle of branches broken by the strokes of a single farmer's hoe, whom one's eye attempts in vain to find among the dense orange trees or the lemon trees, or hidden within the dark, leaden leaves of the olive trees." He sees Monte Solaro, "the great regulator and dike of the sunlight": he knows the "sweetest tremendous solitude" of certain places where "destiny does not touch the earth but remains suspended between heaven and the sea." He sees at "the propitious hour of day" the houses and "gentle gardens" of Capri, and midday in Anacapri: "It is the great noontime, O friends. The spirits of the air, the sea, and the woods rise upon this hour and go in search of amusement." And together with these spirits, to amuse themselves, go Clio, the Muse of history, and the Emperor Augustus, who, before Tiberius, gave lustre and decorum to the island: "You remained here, flowered litter upon the sea," he says, "and there you could see my grave and serious Romans, lying around all day in the sun, near the rock of Monacone." He meets the spirit of Tiberius, come back now as a dog who follows him around as he wanders across the island, and he recalls the *Teleboi* (fabulous harpooners) among the first of these shores' inhabitants; he recalls the monks of the Certosa, and the Saracens who carried away "the women and children under their arms as if they were faggots of wood, to their ships pitching upon the sea in a tempest"; and the corsairs, the soldiers of Murat who battled against the English and Hudson Lowe; the dignitaries of the court of the Queen of Sweden, who "drank coffee on the terrace of the Hotel Paradise. The living and the dead multiply the suggestion of these places." When the image-making voyager goes to the Villa Jovis and faces the Salto di Tiberio, the Leap of Tiberius: "from the depths of that chasm where all sensation of distance disappeared, I felt rising a sweet but insistent question. In the emptiness close by that crag, Death sang with inimitable accents. She spoke in a motherly voice, inspiring faith more than any living being. Who would restrain me from abandoning myself to her?" Finally, through some kind of sorcery, Savinio rushes down a subterranean corridor from the age of Tiberius, down to the Blue Grotto, upon whose vault open and close "countless blue eyes. Other blue eyes likewise stretched before me, but they were so close, so closely knit, that they formed a magic carpet, gently palpitating atop the slow rocking of the calm sea" (and these eyes echo Marinetti's "glances of water").

Upon exiting the Blue Grotto, he ducks his head and climbs aboard a boat, and then leaves the island. "In a short while, surrounded by the boundless sea, I saw the tall phantasm of the Steel Island slowly vanish into night. Farewell. Farewell."

With a masterly change of scene, Savinio completes the "voyage" both real and fantastic in which all places named, turned into popular locations on the Capri itinerary, return to living in their original stupor, redeemed in these few short pages from the humiliation that was imposed on them. In the abundant but frequently mediocre literature on Capri, this small golden book by Alberto Savinio rises like some stone dedicated to the "numinal" island. By eventful good fortune, Capri found a writer of a stature equal to that of her myth.

GOING TO THE
VILLA LYSIS

Each time I climb the Via di Sopramonte, I always remember a time when I came to these parts in order to reach a house that remains in my memory like a dream. I searched so many times without ever finding it, and the one I did find—probably the same place where I stayed—seems so different to me now, because it is so completely in ruins, that I did not recognize it, and I could not connect it with the house of my memories. Perhaps this happens even to our past, among whose ruins everything becomes unrecognizable.

This house was a kind of fortress, rising up in one of the most beautiful and solitary places on Capri, Pian delle Noci, a small high plain covered with a pine forest that ends in a precipice above the Villa Malaparte. If you were carefully to approach the wood's edge, you would see such a headlong drop of rocks above the sea as to make your head spin. From the side near the Natural Arch the pines end at a belvedere that is one of the most extraordinary on this island that seems to be made of belvederes.

In that fortress-villa I lived for a few days many years ago, but in my mind I still see it. Back then I was a youth with many confused ideas in my head, but I was sure that I wanted to make a writer of myself. And by one of those chances that occur sometimes in life, I met and became friends with two writers: one already very famous, Moravia, and the other who would soon become famous, Elsa Morante. Elsa was always most kind to me, perhaps because she always loved young people and identified youth with beauty, idealism, and generosity. And I was not only young but also full of enthusiasm for literature, and I talked and talked, and Elsa laughed at the things I was saying, perhaps because I said them in such an exultant tone, or perhaps because I said things that were neither of heaven nor of earth. I was speaking of literature, and of poetry, about poets I had discovered and was translating. And whenever Elsa introduced me to someone, she called me "the young poet" (and added my name) making me want to hide in embarrassment.

Therefore, young with beautiful hopes, I met Moravia and Morante that year, and I do not know how, for two or three days I found myself in the house I spoke about that they had rented together with an English friend. This friend was in turn a friend of Norman Douglas, the famous Norman Douglas that I saw back then in the curious aspect of a venerable old man who was playing Pygmalion to some child. I was very intrigued by the rapport between the two, also because a classical air hung about them, Norman, tall, with short white hair, and the boy, leaning toward him and asking about this and that. When I saw them I thought of nothing but two figures painted upon a Greek vase.

Sometimes I surprised them absorbed in the contemplation of a landscape, silhouetted against the sky at sunset, and what could they have had to say to each other, I would ask myself, a man almost eighty years old and a thirteen-year-old boy? Douglas was one of the few witnesses still living of that Caprese society during the golden age that Compton Mackenzie described. Was not Douglas a friend and dining companion of Fersen? And had he not, together with Clavel, discussed at the Villa Lysis, at Fersen's table, homosexual love as if in a dialogue of Plato? And was not Douglas always the only one among all of them capable of raising his own aestheticism to higher levels, the only one in whose books one feels at times the inspiration of the travelers of the Grand Tour, of the tradition that had its representatives in Goethe, in De Brosses, in Gissing? And was it not also in him, as in Lawrence, that the exaltation of the spirit and pagan sexuality, and love for the Mediterranean and for Italy, became a way of rebelling against Victorian conformism? All these things made Douglas in my eyes at that time a completely respectable figure, even if I watched him with the detachment with which one looks at the exhibit of a great vanished civilization. So I recalled—as I proceeded, up the Via di Sopramonte and straight to the Villa Lysis—all these things that date back to those years immediately after the war, and I remembered one scene very clearly: Douglas, his head crowned with vine leaves like an old satyr, chasing after Elsa through the woods, partly in play, partly because he had been drinking. And the scene among the trees in the pinewood, in the wild silence of the place, had a magical quality, as if Arcadia had been reborn for a moment on that late afternoon in Capri and one could again sense Pan wandering through the forest. But what I remembered even better was the excited laughter, amused and even a bit frightened, the

childlike titter of the nymph Elsa, who ran among the trees followed by the satyr Norman.

Elsa had a round face with two large eyes with speckled green
irises, full of lights and shadows, small wide-spaced teeth that
were completely visible when she laughed, reminding you, in an
impressionistic way, of the face of a cat. When she laughed with
those tiny teeth all in view, one seemed to see a panting cat, so
much so that at times in my mind I added whiskers to her upper
lip, like a cat's, which seemed to be made of nylon.

Once with Elsa and Alberto we went to find Curzio Malaparte in that villa of his that seems born out of the Caprese
landscape, conferring upon it a curious twentieth-century form.
Malaparte had the beauty of a star of the old cinema, with a
hairstyle as in the black-and-white films of the thirties. He had
an elegant figure and an air part melancholy and part serious
that strangely reminded me of the *saltimbanques* from Picasso's
blue period. His legend and his lifestyle were well adapted to a
Capri where a touch of dandyism and a little extravagance
never failed. He was courteous, but most of all he wished to
seduce, and that time when Elsa, Alberto, and I went to find
him, he showed me his study, where, beneath the windowsill of
a large and grand window curved like the poop of a ship and
facing the sea and the Faraglioni, a library–writing room had
been constructed. Along the bookshelves was a movable chair
upon a track, so that the person seated there could move easily
to this or that side of the landscape, and could get to work in the
position that was most pleasing. From this bookcase he took
out a volume of the *Recherche*, and then *Ulysses*, translated into
French by Valéry Larbaud, and then he told me that he had been
the first in Italy to read those books, and it wickedly occurred to
me that at any rate you didn't find a trace of them in his own

work. He also showed me various rooms in that home-barracks furnished according to the most heterogeneous and contrasting styles and he told me that many of those furnishings were "plunder of war"—he said it exactly like that, "the plunder of war," and I believe that he did it in order to shock me. The bed with the canopy had been seized in Romania, and that stove in Russia, and the chest of drawers in Finland. . . . If I had not been the boy that I was, critical and intransigent to the point of annoyance, I would certainly have been seduced by that snake charmer who left you to imagine who knows what "inimitable life" behind his "plunder of war."

But I had read *La Pelle, The Skin*, and I had my reservations about Malaparte, irremovable reservations, in spite of a certain sympathy that I felt for him and for his vanity. I had read those insipid and prolix dialogues in which an Allied general, high officials, and ladies of high social rank hung on the lips of a charming Malaparte, liaison officer, who at the gambling table held the bank and rattled off, with the air of saying who knows what profound things, one banality after another. And how his table companions enjoyed themselves, how they admired him for his spirit and his inexhaustible verve, how they exploded in uncontainable laughter every time he opened his mouth! Those dialogues in which you could not tell who was more unprepared, the author or his characters, dialogues that proposed again and again the same pathetic opposition between victors and vanquished without ever saying anything interesting on the subject—those I never really managed to forgive him for. How many absurd generalizations did General Cork proclaim, and what an ugly part did Malaparte devise for himself! He seemed like the lapdog of the victors, wagging his tail appropriately when he wished to appear proud. And those Neapolitan nobles, who perhaps in the author's intentions should have come across as "Proustian," succeeded only in being old dotards. And what about the arrival of the siren fish, which was the highlight of the novel, served at table with mayonnaise and surrounded by coral, its arrival preceded and seasoned by lots of idiotic chatter? "Is the coral good to eat?" asked General Cork. Can anyone be more stupid? And then the considerations on the coral and the poor boiled babies, American candor and European ambiguity, the apparitions of the old Neapolitan hags, of the dogs in the vivisection room, and so on. It aroused indignation, in aesthetic disgust, at least I thought so then. But, as you know, the young are ferocious when they pass judgment. Moravia said jokingly, "I don't believe him, even when he is telling the truth."

Instead, the Capresi, in their own way and despite certain misunderstood precedents, had been seduced by Malaparte. Moravia seduced no one. He had been coming to Capri since '36 and he had written some of his most important books on Capri, but he had never become a "personality" here, because in order to become one it is necessary to have a really good dose of the mythomania that Moravia lacked and Malaparte had. And so Malaparte reenters the legend of Capri, together with so many others who exhibited themselves upon its stage; Moravia instead did not and no one ever names him.

Meanwhile, having left the Via di Sopramonte, I penetrated the alleyways of upper Capri that lead to Tiberius, in that miniature Switzerland—quiet and secluded, far from the crowd and the bustle of the piazza—where I was thinking of these things, of those persons, and of the days spent in that house on the Pian delle Noci. I remembered precisely not only the faces of that time but many details and episodes as well. Like the moonlit evening during which we heard a concert of Beethoven in the pinewood: suddenly there was established among us one of those moments in which all our souls seem to harmonize into a single feeling, and each one of us has the same perception of it and receives it with amazement. And right there at that moment two friends of mine arrived from the piazzetta, arguing, a boy and a girl both rivals in love—I was the subject of the dispute—and I saw, in their arrival and in their boldness in showing their feelings for me in front of everyone, a possible catastrophe that could cause me to be forever disdained by my hosts. But in reality they were very amused by the situation and my embarrassment. Thinking of Capri in those days, it seemed to me as though another person must have lived at that time, certainly not I.

With these thoughts and with these memories I reached the end of the road that leads to the fork where one side climbs up to the Villa Jovis and the other, on the left, leads to the Villa Lysis. Here at the fork, the view opens out over a beautiful countryside divided by flat stone walls and gardens and vines and hedges of prickly pears, with the austere ruins of the villa of Tiberius in the background.

The house where Fersen lived can no longer be seen, hidden as it is by a thicket of trees. Before you manage to see it, you have to travel down an access avenue and finally there it is with its columns, its balustraded terraces, its garden that dominates the landscape from on high. The last time I came up here, I was a little late, but, still unwilling to renounce my visit, I arrived as the daylight gave way to evening and in the air was a pale-blue and slightly opalescent luminosity, in which things appeared to be bordered by a dark line and silhouetted. In that light at dusk, as I approached one side of the villa that has a balustrade over a precipice straight down to the sea, I saw a strange figure with a human shape walking like a monkey upon that narrow balustrade in fits and starts, which made me dizzy just watching him. I stood still, holding my breath, feeling that in an unforeseeable and treacherous way, the influence of the place had already seized me. Who was that creature who with the disjointed movements of a puppet danced over the black abyss in the faltering light of the evening? I learned later that the mongoloid son of a custodian had an insane passion for precipices.

Now having reached it some years later at a different and brighter hour, I was able to observe well the villa and its frightful decay since the last time I had been there. I thought, In a few years there will be nothing left here. And with this sensation I drew nearer. Architectonically the villa is pretentious, but it has its dignity. Even if the style is Louis XVI, as the customer and the architect had wished, the final result is Art Nouveau without a doubt. The neoclassical columns, in whose flutings were glimpses of the residue of the ancient gilding, were like the remains of a pathetic and decadent dream that came to Capri in order to die. But in Fersen's own death, more than in his life or in his work, there is a kind of fatality, or at least the sign of a destiny lived out to its final consequences. If it is true, as Cocteau said, that Fersen, like Ludwig of Bavaria, belongs to that type of decadent or aesthete who, being incapable of creating a masterpiece, wishes to make a masterpiece of himself and of his own life, Fersen's own attempt was, to the end, his own tragic seriousness. Even the villa he had built on Capri must have played a part in this project, and I, on that day, was wandering around in what remained of that dream.

The rooms of the Villa Lysis are all in a state of ruin and indescribable neglect, everything is decrepit, all rotted, crumbling. Of that villa of an earlier time you still recognize the facade with its columns and the upper terrace with its balustrade; not much remains of the much praised grand staircase with the railing of bronze vine leaves; you barely see the outline of the rooms and the shape of the opium den situated in a strategically perfect manner in respect to the view. All things considered, I do not think that this villa was such a great thing even during the height of its splendor, but not even I would define it, as Cocteau did, as bric-a-brac in a modern Greco-pre-Raphaelite style. And I believe that, after all, restoring it would be worthwhile. The island's enchantment was always in this encounter between nature and history—indeed, and more often, between nature and mythomania—that is manifested here more than elsewhere. The history is the grandiose history of Tiberius, which time, as it does with all things, has erased down to the very stones. The mythomania is the more modest one of so many lives that landed here and knew passions, had dreams, lived illusions, and expressed in many ways that Mediterranean licentiousness then in vogue.

The earthly existence of this little Ludwig of Capri who built the Villa Lysis, even in his narcissistic-aestheticizing obviousness, has its perfection befitting a legend. Yes, it was far from Capri, in old Europe, the "cultural" origin of so many dreams that came here to die while they believed they were being born; and perhaps this is why at times Capri makes me think of Böcklin's celebrated painting, entitled *The Island of the Dead*. Böcklin's atmosphere emerges from many spots on Capri, and certainly I felt it as I entered the garden of the Villa Lysis, hanging above the sea, beyond the little bridge, before the small neoclassical temple and the belvedere, in the silence of the hour that precedes evening.

ROMANTIC MONIKA

When one has arrived here, in front of the house of Monika Mann, the piazza, the crowd in Capri, the continuous bustle of the tourists, all seem so far away, so remote. There is only the solemn and magnificent view of the Faraglioni, the cry of the gulls, and the infinite sea. In a certain sense, this view is untenable, I tell Monika Mann, in order to break the ice. How could she endure it here for thirty years?

The lady is not in the mood and she does not answer me. I think she is not happy with these visits. Too much news in the newspapers, too many photos, too much noise. Now is a difficult moment for her; it all happened so fast. Antonio, the man she lived with for many years, has died. He awoke one night, said that he had chest pain, breathed deeply three times, and then died. Not even enough time to call a doctor. And now it is impossible for her to live here alone. She must leave Capri, quickly, in a few days. Here, she would wish for a little tranquility around her. "But is there something the papers have written that displeases you?" She seems distracted, thinking of something else. "What is a newspaper? It lasts a day, then it is gone." She is very confused, she says as an excuse. I ask other questions, attempting to start up the conversation. "I don't know, I don't know my future. Everything is utopia." She means to say that everything is uncertain. Hers is a special Italian; she speaks it in her own way. And meanwhile she wrings her hands continuously with an anguished movement.

She is thin, delicate, frail, her face resembles her father's. If she had the mustache and the straw hat, she would be identical to him. . . . Her father wrote in a letter, "Monika is a psychically fragile creature . . . that poor little one must have suffered atrocious things." He was alluding to the wreck of the ship that was carrying Monika and her husband to America in 1940, just after they had been married. The ship was sunk by the Germans, her husband died, she was saved. Again Mann writes (in a letter to his friend Feuchtwanger), "Monika arrived here with paralyzed hands because she had to grab hold of the side of a broken boat for twenty hours." Those same hands were now writhing in anguish before me, and they did not know what to do.

The room in which we are talking, I realize, is simply furnished, with a touching poverty I would call Franciscan. Everything is in neat order, clean, but it is really the minimum. A folding bed with a mattress and a woolen blanket, a mirror resting upon the floor, the desk, a table, a chair, a small armchair. The only luxurious things in this bare simplicity are complete editions of the works of Thomas Mann, the first edition and all those that followed, rebound and arranged with care.

She says that she is very tired this morning, perhaps the heat. The heat is terrible today. The conversation does not proceed. Then I have an idea: I ask her for her book, the last she wrote. I will skim through it there outside, I tell her, and I will return later to speak with her. If she feels like it.

"Yes, I lived my childhood in a house full of movement, and its sound and its ringing is still loud in my memory . . . brothers, sisters, servants, animals, . . . the outside world seemed to be reflected in our house, not just because a great number of travelers arrived there, but as a result of my father's character. Even if he lived concentrating upon himself, his mind was always open to the world. However, I soon realized that in every artist there is something like a *non-life* . . . I belong to a family that as far back as I can recall was guided by this *non-life*. It was like a ghost who crossed through the house. . . ."

Monika wrote this in the book I am leafing through. I stand there with the book in my hands, in front of her house, where there is a little belvedere in the shade of the trees. The book is dedicated *To Toni*. On the first page I read, "My father died on August 12, 1955. I signed with a cross the page I was writing when the news reached me." And in fact on page 111, I found the cross. This father is always present, page after page she speaks of him, he must have been an idée fixe; but you come to understand that they saw and spoke to each other rarely, and there must have been a great distance between him and his children. Just now the singing of the birds can be heard among the trees, notwithstanding the loud crying of the gulls. A supersonic jet is engulfed by the blue of the sky, leaving a long white vapor trail. I have been reading for an hour. I take some notes. I hear her voice over my shoulder, and her curious Italian. "Are you creative?" which I translate as "Are you working? Am I disturbing you?" She sits beside me, wearing a silk blouse and a pair of yellow slacks. Her white hair is carefully combed.

"Do you know that you remind me a little of Musil?"

"Really?"

"Yes, you resemble him." She chuckles. "A very similar head."

She changed her mood. A while ago she was tense, nervous. Now it is she who is talking to me.

"He courted you?"

"Yes. We met in Zurich."

"What was Musil like?"

"He was quite small. . . . He was very unhappy because his fame in the world was not great enough. But how could it be? He wrote too little to have the great fame he wished for."

"*The Man Without Qualities* is an important book, however. That fame has finally been granted to him. He wrote little because what he wanted was nearly impossible."

"Have you read *The Man Without Qualities*?"

"Yes, certainly."

"I haven't." She laughs, covering her mouth with her hand. "I haven't read much by him. Almost nothing. But it didn't matter to him."

"Was he really in love with you?"

"He even wrote it somewhere, I don't know where: Monika . . . Monika . . . Monika . . ."

"And why have you never read him? Didn't you like him? Or did you find him too intellectual?"

"Too intellectual." And she laughs as if caught in the act.

"In your book you speak of a *non-life* of the artist, and it seems that this scares you. Were you alluding to your father?"

She doesn't answer. At times, more often than not understanding, it seems that she is not listening.

"Upon reading your book, one sees that you have great admiration for your father, respect, but that, in short, the distance that he put between himself and others was hard also for you."

Perhaps she is distracted again, or she did not hear. She looks out at the sea. But then in a breath she says, "I think that the intellect is something that gets in the way. . . . There is no direct relation with all of this." And she indicates the expanse of the sea.

"Therefore you prefer simple folk?"

"Yes, they are closer to everything."

"Antonio was like that?"

"He was like that, but he did not know it. Musicians are also like that. They are close to everything."

"Do you like music?"

"Oh, yes, very much." She likes Mozart most of all. One time after the death of her father, she was listening to Mozart, and she had the terrible perception of his nonexistence. "Listening to music is a very singular feeling, it can make you feel as if struck by a thunderbolt and flung to earth." That time as she listened to Mozart, the fact that her father could no longer listen to his music filled her with the unbearable consciousness of his nonexistence. It was a strong feeling that lasted only an instant. "I tried to seize it, it was an electric shock, a sadness that penetrated me, and already it had flown off into the darkness like some demon. I almost fainted."

She rises. "Now I am going to take my walk. Would you like to keep me company?" And so our walk begins. From Monika's house, proceeding along the little street of Pizzolungo, there is a stretch thick with trees and shade, very cool. On one side the rock face, on the other the precipice, and at the bottom, between the branches of trees and the myrtle bushes, you can glimpse the blue sea. After barely fifty meters, there are some stairs that climb up, and there Monika's walk ends. Turning around, she returns toward the house. Then again turning around, as far as the stairs. And so on for a good many times, until completing the distance of a kilometer or more. This walk Monika takes two or three times a day, in order to stay in shape. She takes small steps, as older persons do. She used to take it with Antonio, who had heart disease and needed to move about. Toni, she tells me, was not a fisherman, as the newspapers had reported. He was a master mason. "With his father he built our house. He was very good with his hands. He made so many things. He made a blue grotto all illuminated with blue light, beautiful, and inside tiny boats that moved around, and there was even music, like a carillon. Then he made sailing ships with sails and everything, and he made ships in bottles and sold them to the tourists."

"But were you two always alone, in this house?"

"Sometimes we had visitors. He had two friends from here."

"But weren't you together too much?"

"He had the floor below and I had the upper floor, each had his own life."

"But then . . ."

"Each other's presence was enough. We were very much united, even if he said that I was like the fruit on the prickly pear, outside covered with thorns but sweet on the inside. He built the blue grotto, I listened to Mozart. Why did we need to speak?"

"During winter here, in this part of the island, it must be terrible when the wind is beating down and there is a storm."

"I like the winter a lot. I prefer the winter, with our little stove, to the summer. Sometimes there are certain waves down below, tremendous waves, and when the sea is too rough the taste of salt reaches up here. I taste it in my mouth, because the wind carries it up with the spray."

"In winter do you still take your walk? Do you ever go down to the piazzetta to sit and have coffee?"

"Sometimes, but usually we stayed here. We were always here. There's a friend of Toni's who does our shopping for us."

"Don't these fifty meters of the world seem rather few to you?"

"It's so beautiful. You walk as if upon the deck of a ship. The ship is moving as you walk. The ship is the fantasy. And then the people pass by, some tourists, and if they are Germans I delight in hearing their accents, if one is from Monaco I talk to him. One has encounters. . . . Then there are the gulls, do you see them up there? I know each of them. And the birds. . . . And there is a family of mice in the trees. . . ."

"They wouldn't be squirrels by any chance?"

"There are no squirrels on Capri. They are mice. Mother, father, and three little ones. They eat pine nuts. They split open the cones with their teeth and they eat the pine nuts. During the night Toni and I used to listen to them. We listened in the silence to their crack-crack until dawn, and in the morning we found the empty pinecones. They ate so many of them."

"Everyone is different, I understand. But under this indifferent sky I would not know how to withstand thirty years in a solitude like this."

"If the sky could show us sympathy, what would become of us? Isn't it really its indifference that puts our feelings into motion?"

"When you came to Capri and met Antonio, how much time had passed since your husband's death?"

"Fifteen years. I came from America. I didn't know where to go."

"What do you recall about the sinking?"

"On the train to Liverpool, before embarking, we saw a boy and a girl. He was in uniform. They were so sad, because he was leaving for the front and they had to part. I sensed that their destiny was also our own. We boarded the ship, and that voyage was our honeymoon voyage."

We had walked back and forth many times as we talked. Now we enter the house. The house that Antonio built is high above the Faraglioni; there are only two or three others with this view. Its architecture is genuine, rustic Caprese, with its arches, its columns, the little terraces, some pointed-arch windows, and whitewashed walls. But as soon as I enter, I am again struck by the extreme poverty of its furnishings, although everything expresses dignity. It must be a choice, I believe, because Monika, with the rights to her father's works, certainly doesn't have money problems. While she goes to change her shoes (as she always does after her walk) I see one of Antonio's blue grottoes. It is a box with a little scene inside; but without the light and the music, and without any movement, it is like a firefly seen during the daytime beneath a glass, it has no magic. The sailboat is better, with its rigging, and so is an island of Capri, sculpted in relief and framed. Upon the wall I observe a watercolor with a human figure. *A Pageant* is written below, a kind of actor. Monika has returned. "Kokoschka did that," she tells me as if she were talking about one of Antonio's works. "He also painted the cupboard in the kitchen."

"Did Kokoschka come here often?"

"He came to see us many times when he stayed on Capri. He liked this house, and Toni's company. He also painted on the terrace. He used to say that it was beautiful here. But he knew that it is necessary to come to terms with beauty, that it is not necessary to conquer her, to understand that she does not permit herself to be dominated." As she speaks, she becomes angry with herself. "I lack so many words; I have been here thirty years and still I haven't learned to speak. . . ."

Upon the road, as I return to the piazzetta, I ask myself if this woman was happy. This island, Antonio, were they the pieces of wood to which she clung in the shipwreck of her life? And now that her hands have had to abandon their grasp, what will become of her? Later at home, I reread this excerpt that I sight-translated from her book and wrote down:

Autumn has arrived on my island. One hardly notices because the sun is hot, only a golden shadow has been added to its blinding splendor. The prickly pear is at the height of its glory, and bunches of grapes swollen with juice hang down from the vines. The air has become a bit more still, even though the wind blows forcefully at times, and there is something more coy about the dawn, it doesn't seem like a greeting to all humanity. People become rare and soon no one will be seen here, and we will be by ourselves among these rocks, watching the sea below. We will go hunting for dried wood for our stove, to shout our names at the wind, and when the sun sets and the clouds of winter are ablaze in the west like an Angelus, we will tremble with them in a single heartbeat. And the sound of the bells will rise. But everything is distant, even the bell ringer is far off and we are here alone on the island. As we return home a branch becomes entangled with my hair; we stop walking, try to disentangle it, you are laughing, I am laughing too, we have to hurry, it is getting dark. The dried wood burns in the hearth, the night consumes everything around us. . . . During the winter the island seems uninhabited, the inhabitants enclose themselves within the two towns, the one high above, the other lower down, the fishermen go off in their boats to Naples to sell their fish. In the morning, we watch them disappear in the distance. We watch them from the curve in the road where you can see Malaparte's house push out into the sea like a red ship. We hold on to each other, facing each other above the precipice, we watch the waves, green beneath the cliffs and blue where the gulls are flying. They hover in the air with wings still, like the falcons and eagles, they scan the surface of the sea and suddenly dive down, falling with a cry. It is no longer solitary here. The sea pounds around the island like some visitor who arrives from far away, and all Capri is a tall, shining fortress in the middle of an agitated world. . . . Then we lean out to look at two lizards dancing in the sun.

IMAGES OF THE ISLAND

On a mild summer evening, carrying a sleeping bag and a bottle of the local white wine, my friend Luciano (Luciano D'Alessandro, *Vivere Capri*, Guida: Napoli, 1988), a photojournalist who usually is sent to the front line of the world's hot spots, climbs to the summit of Monte Solaro to await the first light of dawn: he has a date. He wants to surprise Capri as she awakens, to capture her when daybreak's rose fingers tint the sky with their soft colors. The attempt is not successful, because the bottle of wine is a traitor and sleep persists longer than expected. But the following evening, with a more frugal partaking of the bottle, his mission is successful. Luciano awakes at the right hour, arrives punctually for his date, and the outcome of that amorous encounter between the island and himself is an image shot by him in which you see Capri still dotted with lights, the rosy streak of the sunrise separating her from the sky. In the upper right corner, a crescent moon and Venus, the shining morning star.

If it is so that the gods who once inhabited these places are now gone, it is also true that sometimes, at a more propitious place and hour, they return for a brief appearance and you can still hope to encounter them as you do the migrating birds. Luciano is this type of hunter. Here on Capri he goes hunting for numinous images and sometimes, with a little ability and luck, he captures one.

There is a kind of leaden melancholy that runs through Luciano's images of Capri, a barely discernible tension, and I believe this melancholy is due not only to those other images (of war, pain, suffering) that make up his usual work and are perhaps impressed forever into his gaze, but also because whoever comes to Capri for many years knows that here too it is necessary to resign yourself to the Inevitable and the Irreversible. He knows that all places delegated by Beauty, all terrestrial paradises, have been found to be violated and desecrated and there is no escape. He knows that Capri is one of these and it is necessary to put into play, even here, a special strategy for inventing your own island within the island. But, even so, it is not possible to avoid that particular depression, the melancholy that overtakes us, when we realize how this island is being consumed every day.

In what does Luciano's "special strategy" consist? First of all, in knowing—in order to avoid them—the schedules and itineraries of the groups escorted here by the Terrible Tourist Agencies, the arrivals of the ferryboats and their departures, the hour when the proprietors of the motorboats roar out of the port and the hour when everybody departs together, finally leaving the sea free; and you need to know the rocks where the sun beats down the longest and how to find a boat at the right moment, the restaurants to frequent and which dishes to request, the atmospheric events foreseeable in the day and the changes in the winds, without neglecting astronomy, the nights of the full moon and of the starry sky.

With this knowledge it is not difficult to create a vital space for oneself, one's own territory, or even one's own Natural Park. It is enough to find a rhythm of life contrary to that of the over-whelming majority of the island's occupants, habituating one-self to a counter-schedule that will seem at times even a little strange or tiresome or impractical, but that in the end will repay whoever employs it. The special conformation of the island is helpful, for three-quarters of her is impervious and inaccessible and for this reason, and this reason only, is in large part unin-jured by the curse of the automobiles that rage on Ischia or along the Amalfi coast. Long, solitary walks are therefore still possible even during the busiest days, when the invasion seems at its peak. As soon as one distances oneself, if only by a few meters, from the stream of tourists, one discovers here a differ-ent Capri, with its own parallel existence, completely indifferent to that of its incidental guests.

Luciano passes to me the photographs he shot, which have an almost narrative rhythm. The tourists arrive! And the pictures show them while in gushes, in bunches, in an avalanche, they pour from the bridge of the ferryboat, heading for the stairways, pouring out onto the quay. Then the usual destinations and the usual tolls: the Blue Grotto, and the filled-up boats that float upon a liquid light, waiting. Other boats that venture out for the "tour of the island" and are seen again from above, tiny as ants beneath the vertical rocks, in order to underline the crush-ing disproportion between nature looming here and the noth-ingness of the human presence. Boats will proceed with their cargo from one inlet to the next, violating the solitude of the most hidden recesses, of the gorges where the reflections of light on the water and the marine transparencies will cross, sounding the entire gamma of greens and blues.

How different from these little pilgrims' boats are those of the rich, who remain to idle about lazily at the pier! When their private engines break the public silence and they begin to grind up the blue sea, on the close-packed surface there will appear white semicircles of foam drawn by their wakes, and like the eye of a falcon the lens will have caught and fixed them in a photogram before they disappear.

Later, everybody will find themselves in the piazzetta, ready to play at *mirar y ser mirado*, seeing and being seen, in front of an ice-cream or a glass more beautiful to gaze at than to drink from, dressed up with fruit and colors like a Brazilian during Carnival in Rio.

During the summer, the Capresi leave the piazzetta to the tourists; only the young are there, the others prefer to remain in their homes, which are always pretty and welcoming, even the poorer ones. Luciano knows everybody here; he has managed to enter many homes of every kind, of Capresi and of residents, and he has always done it as if on tiptoe, the unobserved guest, with an alert gaze, and it is through his eyes that I now see these interiors, I feel the atmosphere that he breathes there. And here is Fersen's house, a house in ruins. The windows with rotted shutters and the corroded walls belong to a mysterious house of Usher that the lens has surprised as the reflection of a dying sun illumines the arches of the lower floor, and it seems that an entire epoch has faded here at the Villa Lysis.

Foreshortenings of roads, alleys, narrow underground passages, and crooked stairways, entrances, someone standing at a window watching time and life pass by, a nun entering a lobby, a whisper of evening voices, a name, a call, murmuring around a corner. . . . One can see and hear the hidden village where a little ancient world still lives, just a few steps from the grand modern hotels and the boutiques on Via Camerelle. Here the architecture of the place has fashioned sweet tangles of arches and volutes among the whitewashed walls and the welcome shade of a Casbah.

The photos I am looking at speak of all this, and of the churches with swelling cupolas like rising dough, with bell towers that ring the hour with ceramic numerals, and of the ruins of the Certosa, the color of biscuits; they tell of everything that happens in this little ancient world, the feast of the patron saint and of the Madonna of the Libera in the Marina Grande, processions, a marriage, a first communion as naive as a Rousseau painting. . . . Outside, distant, indifferent to this humanity, the island lives in her own eternal time, among magnificent landscapes, peaks, rocks, romantic solitudes. And how much my friend, this image hunter, must have walked in order to express his feeling before such an overexposed view! Sometimes, however, he managed to overcome the barrier of the already seen, and to reveal, outside the models already noted and consumed, the beauty of this island with little, modest shots, as if fearing that he too would contribute to the wear and tear of the panorama, would exploit it, he too, while believing he was celebrating it.

The Sorrentine Peninsula, seen from Monte Tiberio, from Matromania, from the Pian delle Noci, or the small Roman port of Tragara, seen from a belvedere high above, always seems to be suspended in an hour, in an instant, in an unusual and true moment. And here is a photograph that could have been invited to an exhibition on futurism, because it is a small masterpiece where form, geometry, and movement achieve perfect harmony, or, as they used to put it, "dynamic." It is the madhouse of

Malaparte, seen as an Aztec pyramid for sacrificing to the Mediterranean sun, and shot while, in the deep-blue background of the sea, a speedboat passes, leaving behind a spray and a wake like the tail of Halley's comet. One photograph like this is enough to evoke all the Marinettis, Bragaglias, Deperos, Clavels, and Cangiullos, who were tourists here on Capri, or, rather, futurists, who in the piazzetta futurized a future of automobiles, airplanes, velocipedes, and other dynamic deviltries that, alas, we have now learned to appreciate, we and not they!

Even when it is not seen, the sea here at Capri is always present, and renders this island drunk like Rimbaud's drifting boat. The blue-green incandescent sea, luminous or illuminated, transparent in the net of the incandescent sun, streaked with scales of coagulated azure, foaming with whitecaps, according to the mood of the winds; the winds that furrow the sea and make it change, the sirocco wind and the *maestrale*, the *libeccio* and the *ponente*, each with its own waves, each with its own light. And as the light changes with the changes in the wind, so too does the light change and startle within the photographs that Luciano shows me.

Of the sunrise in shades of pink I have already spoken, but the last shot is that of Capri at twilight, just as if seen from the height of my house, a Capri of the thousand and one nights, dotted with lights, moving like a ship, upon the sea, *"infuso d'astri e lattescente,"* drowned in stars and milky white, where Siren Land fades into the violet evening.

THE SPIRITS OF
THE PLACE

It can happen on Capri that at a certain hour of the day, in a certain place, on a certain occasion, one of the spirits that looks after a grotto, a cliff, a forest, or a rock appears unexpectedly in an unforeseeable shape, as a feeling or stupor, pathos or fear, suddenly taking possession of you. At times Capri seems like the mysterious island; the island of voices. There are nights in which, given the particular conditions of the winds, of the earth's atmosphere, of the sky's currents and the sea's currents, from the *Grotta delle Felci*, not far as the crow flies from my house—there where prehistoric people once lived, and where it is still possible to discover flints, earthenware, and bones—there emerges a kind of sigh, an immense sigh, a kind of *Aaaaaaah* smothered, but which is heard and expands distinctly in the surrounding space, as if a great wild beast, a wounded antediluvian monster, were weeping or about to give out its last breath. And it seems that a farmer or an old countrywoman from this part of the world knows exactly and in advance when this phenomenon will be produced, on the basis of what signs or premonitions no one knows. Not more than two or three years ago, the sound was repeated so often that groups of people went in the evening to a place near the grotto to listen to that lament, and some attributed it to the souls of the victims of human sacrifices that were once carried out in the grotto, some to complex meteorological occurrences, but all were struck by such an anguished sound.

On some evenings, I sit on my terrace with my ears open, especially if there is a great silence all around and I sense the bewitched atmosphere that at times the nights of Capri exhale— either because of the effect of the moon, or because of the starry sky bent over the jagged summit of Monte Solaro, or because the inevitable horned owl makes his warning call at regular intervals—I am there on the terrace and I await the arrival of the great sigh that the people here call *il fiatone*, the big breath. And Eliot's lines come to me: *"This is the way the world ends / Not with a bang but a whimper."* And I imagine that sound, and I almost seem to hear it, like the lament of offended Nature.

It can also happen that, on a little island like this, someone who risks too much to explore its peaks and the rocks stretching out over the sea, if only to take a photograph, disappears forever as if swallowed into nothingness, and not even the corpse is ever recovered, ending up in who knows which inaccessible gorge, or broken up. Just this happened some years ago to a German who went out for a walk and never returned to his hotel. They searched for him for days; his wife and brother came from Germany, they put up posters on the walls of Capri with his picture, asking the question, "Have you seen him?" Nothing, vanished into air. And when I hypothesized a story in the manner of Pirandello's *The Late Mattia Pascal*, they told me that in the last ten years it had happened two other times, in fact, to two women from Capri whom everyone knew. One had gone off to cut the grass upon the mountainside, and another, a spinster, had gone to see a friend. In both cases, notwithstanding the searches in the places where they had been seen for the last time, the bodies were never found, or any other trace: they too vanished into thin air.

Yes, this island is full of mysteries and strange things. So too says the fisherman with the goiter whom I have hired in order to take a ride. It seems that no one knows on which nights in which seasons, in certain gorges, grottoes, or inlets, swarms of fish, needlefish, fall so deeply in love that the male and the female twist together and form a knot that no one can undo, and there is a person who swears that he collected some dead ones upon the shore, still embracing each other in their love knot.

We are passing in front of the Baths of Tiberius and the water is deep, almost blue-violet. Here the rock is extremely steep, coming precipitously down in a straight drop from Anacapri, a precipice of some hundreds of meters, frightening. Here and there, a few dwarf palms cling to it, but are beautifully shaped, like natural bonsai. The boatman follows my gaze and tells me that a few days ago a boy who was calmly talking with his friends ran off and threw himself over the precipice. And, being Caprese, unconsciously resurrecting his atavistic mistrust in the Anacapresi (who are "less emancipated," so he says), he touches his head with his hand, as if to say that all those Anacapresi are a little crazy. Every once in a while one of them jumps, at least three or four suicides each year. I call to his attention that Anacapri's inhabitants must be seven thousand, give or take, and that such a percentage of suicides would be too high. But he swears that it is true, and that even if you doubt the story about the needlefish, there can be no doubt that all the Anacapresi are a bit crazy. For example, he knows a certain farmer who shows up on the main road every day going for a walk with his cow, conversing with her the whole time, as if she were his wife. And there is another one, a landowner, who drives at top speed through the little alleyways of Anacapri in a Ferrari that he bought after selling his house and land, a red Ferrari.

But the Capresi do not joke either, and many stories about them are often told. Stories of treasures belonging to Turks hidden in grottoes, and of Tiberius, who every so often returns to life, as when, all aroused, he pursued the beautiful Carmela who lived near the Villa Jovis. One night they found her crazily running and shouting among the ruins, fleeing the assault of that impenitent emperor. Thank God that they then erected an enormous statue of the Madonna there—all out of proportion, as disproportionate as were the sins of Tiberius that it had to outweigh—and everything returned to order: everything except the beauty of the place, which was irremediably compromised. However, the most interesting stories about the Capresi are not ancient but modern ones, about when and how this or that person made his fortune, in hotels, villas, houses, and blows with his fists. Then Capri becomes a tiny *Dallas*, full of the affairs of families ferociously engaged in eternal competition over a square meter of real estate: fathers, sons, heredity, matrimony and patrimony, destinies, hatreds, enemies, lovers, deaths, jealousies, all subject to the law of the Square Meter, single, divine, sacred, inviolate.

But, returning to the mysteries of this island, its very structure is mysterious. It is impossible to imagine a similar geological tangle where such a quantity of points of view is concentrated in such a tiny space. Capri is capricious, labyrinthine; it winds around itself and contorts in a thousand insidious ways. It is enough to surrender even a little to its enticements and the same spot will show itself one time with this face, and another time with a totally different face, because its shape and even its landscape lay traps. And it is known that every labyrinth conceals its minotaur.

Often, I too sensed, walking in some solitary spot at whatever hour of the day or night, something like a magnetic field, an estrangement, forming around a peak or a crag, an indefinable tension in the air in anticipation of some occurrence, in fact a sensation very similar to the one described in the film *Picnic at Hanging Rock*, where a demon suddenly appears out of the earth and entangles, swallows, or destroys the one who by chance falls into its enchantment. Sometimes I have felt the evening climbing over me along the steps excavated between the terraces of an olive grove leading to my house, isolated in the country under Solaro. And stopping every so often to catch my breath, I made out through the branches of the olive trees the powerful sides of the mountain that rose up before me straight against the sky, and I saw they were white with a phosphorous and unreal light that seemed to radiate from the rock itself.

It was not the moonlight that made them look like that, because there was no moon; it could not have been the stars' reflections or those of the inhabitants' lights, because they lived too far away. And in my heart I believed the farmer was right when he told me that the rock of this mountain is a living thing, and in certain special moments it comes alive and it cries, and at times it throws out rocks. It loosens and rolls boulders that crush trees and houses; at times it manifests itself more benignly, emanating the particular light that surprised me.

My daughter Alessandra must have truly seen the face, hidden among the stones of Monte Solaro, of the demon that appeared to the young girls on that walk up Hanging Rock. It was when, my prohibition notwithstanding, she ventured with a boyfriend into the Passetiello. This is the forest that clambers over the steepest side of Solaro, in the direction of the Marina Grande, which takes the name Monte Cappello, and climbs it to reach the plateau of Cetrella at Anacapri. It was by this pathway, considered to be impassable even by the goats, that in 1808 the English, with the help of a rifleman, succeeded in fleeing from the French troops of Murat who had landed on the western shore of Capri. The undertaking, which proved the French victorious, was recounted by Colletta in his beautiful *History of the Kingdom of Naples*, and recently was retold with an abundance of detail by Roberto Ciuni. The path of the Passetiello is indicated by red signs traced upon the rocks, but one easily gets lost because they are too distant from each other. Therefore people often mistake the way, and this is a great risk. At first one comes to a thick vegetation of oaks, holm oaks, chestnuts, strawberry trees, and one walks enclosed in their shade; then one enters a thicket of trees with shorter trunks, myrtles, mastic trees, junipers, which must be pushed aside in order to clear a pathway; finally, the vegetation thins out and the incline gradually increases. If he loses his way, the climber is not aware (thanks to the undergrowth) that the path winds around a large spur of rock, and that at that point, if by chance he were to turn around and look behind him, he would see a horrible abyss that drops straight down for hundreds of meters. Until that moment Alessandra had been climbing with confidence, easily following her friend, not knowing that they had mistaken the way and never imagining the trap that the mountain was preparing for her. Then she turned her head; she saw the chasm behind her and stopped, paralyzed with vertigo and fear. The wall in front of her suddenly seemed smooth and flat and without any ledge, and maybe it really was like that. Her friend, being taller than she, found one grip, then another, never looked back, and with effort managed to reach the summit. He shouted to her from above to wait, and then went off in search of a rope. But the houses of Anacapri are far off, and it requires some time for him to return! Alessandra remains there, suspended on the cliff, with her fingers grasping a hold, and waits. During spring the days are short and it soon begins to get cold up there. The evening shadows are already flying like bats among the fissures of the cliff, and one of those shadows pins her down while desperation enters her heart. A face as smooth and impassible as the wall of rock appears to her, and Alessandra is hypnotized by it. Will it let her go? Will it be unrelenting, as had already happened innumerable times? Or does it want to play with her, like a cat with a mouse? Beneath that gaze of stone a kind of sleepiness takes possession of her, and she swears that she fell asleep. She slept and dreamed of finding in the wall a tiny ledge that she had not seen before. She pulled herself up, leaning upon it, and then—she does not even know how—she reached the summit. Maybe the demon was distracted, maybe he too had fallen asleep. Who knows? These things happen on this island.

Instead, when I climbed for the first time through the Passetiello, I was lucky and quickly found the right path. As I climbed, the dark and damp wooded part reminded me of the threatening undergrowth in the film *Deliverance*. I saw a wild rabbit that I mistook for a hare—but there are no hares on Capri—I passed between two large spurs of rock that seemed like two towers, and when I was above them, stupefied, I looked down at the panorama at the bottom and the sea outstretched like a transparent film over the submerged rocks, and finally I found myself in an Ariostean bower, all green and filled with yellow flowers. There was a silence and a strong feeling of peace; there were no houses nearby and nothing to make you think that this was a tiny island, beaten by the incessant waves of tourists. It seemed, rather, like finding oneself in a mysterious hermit land, as in *Lost Horizon*. I was walking happily in this solitary little valley when I discovered here and there, between the grass and flowers that I was treading upon, the red cartridges of hunters. And after a while I saw them. They were advancing in an open line, like the first line of combat in a kind of Vietnam into which I suddenly seemed to have fallen. The air was full of birds chirruping, but the sky was a smooth and solid blue, like silk, and not a single flight was furrowing it. And that chirruping was not real but a recording, serving as a lure, originating from a small portable tape recorder of the men who were advancing with their rifles pointed toward me.

THE SOLITARY
HOUSE

One evening just before sunset I paid a visit to the Solitaria, the white house that can be seen high upon the cliffs that overhang the Faraglioni, the columns of its circular little loggia projecting out over the wall of the precipice. But it is one thing to see it from the sea in the glitter of the morning and quite another to go there at the beginning of evening, by way of the deserted little alley of Pizzolungo, as the trees' shadows make it even darker. A deep silence marked occasionally by the whir of a bird enwraps everything, and at that hour the Solitary House seems truly to deserve its name. I had been told that beneath the house, hidden among the crags above the little cove of Tragara, there is a tomb excavated from the rock and covered with the magnificent bas-relief of an ancient sarcophagus, which cannot be seen from anywhere, neither from the sea nor from the road, so that it is necessary to go to the spot itself in order to see it. The radiologist Mario Bertolotti, of Turin, who had bought the house in '29, had the tomb built for himself and his family, and afterward obtained permission to do so. It doesn't happen every day that it is possible to visit a house "with a beautiful garden in the style of an amphitheater and a tomb with an exclusive view of the Faraglioni"; and it was precisely this curiosity that guided my steps that evening toward the Casa Solitaria. And there was also the interest awakened within me by the beautiful *Guide to Capri—Capri, la natura e la storia*—written by the present owner, the archaeologist Romana De Angelis, wife of the physicist Mario Bertolotti, the eponymous grandson of the radiologist. A mutual friend had informed me of a terrible misadventure that had struck them; their only daughter was recently killed, in a tragic circumstance, and had also been interred in the family crypt. I knew all this, and still I was unprepared for the sadness that I saw in the black pupils of the mother and in the clear gray and slightly absent eyes of her husband as they received me into their home. From the first, it made my visit embarrassing. My "touristic" curiosity seemed inconvenient and almost vulgar before so much contained grief. I felt like someone who had arrived at the wrong moment, and was about to say that I would abandon my visit. But the gentle reception and the detached simplicity in the manner of my hosts—whom I met there for the first time—convinced me to stay. And so it was that after a little while we went down to the tiny *cimetière marin*.

We went down by a narrow winding path, through a landscape of tumultuous rocks, among spires, peaks, and embattlements extending down into the blue sea, which from that unusual perspective appeared caught between the Faraglioni like some Alpine lake between mountains. This rock amphitheater of gradually descending circles came to be called "the garden" by the Signora, and in its own way it was. Here and there were trees and flowers, and even some rare plants, copies and remains of Greek and Roman statues, amphorae arranged along the way, and even a small temple of Cretan design that we came upon around a bend. Stone benches were placed at the most spectacular views, all of them dizzying, but extraordinary, because at bottom the idea of this hanging garden was simple and evocative and consisted in rendering practicable, and comfortably accessible, a course through precipitous and impervious rocks that only a goat or an ibex would have been able to run along. There you found yourself in a kind of eagle's nest, suspended like a trampoline above the void, where one might sit quietly and observe the view. From there you could make out the other belvederes of the garden, similar to ours, like balconies extending over the abyss, and the surrounding space was so immense that the little iron railing seemed inadequate to establish a secure line of demarcation between the infinite and whoever faced it. The entire scenery of rock was then offered to view; toothed profiles of iguanas and dinosaurs stood silhouetted in black against the colorless pallor of the evening sky, and when the husband of the Signora, who had gone ahead of us, appeared leaning at the railing of another lookout nearby, he too seemed a stone figure cut out against the sky, absorbed, as if bent down by the weight of an extreme solitude.

Beneath us, much farther down, the gulls flew over the blue surface of the sea and over the peaks of the Faraglioni. We saw from above the upper parts of the birds' backs with wings open and still, and this view seemed to augment the height of the place.

"We don't love the seagulls," said the Signora in a sad voice, without intonation. "They have gotten into the habit of coming to our terrace because there is a little marble basin filled with water. They come to refresh themselves and they make such a racket that in order to try and disperse them I had to remove the basin. You do not know how mad they became! For days they protested by beating their beaks against the windowpanes until I put the basin back. I do not like them. . . ."

"You do not see many of them, however."

"It depends on the season. For about ten years, those large ones with a wingspan of two meters have been coming. They are royal gulls. They come from the north, from Norway, and they migrate along the coast of Africa."

"Do they nest here too?"

"Why not? One day, right here near the crypt, I found four newborn gulls. They nested there, and our little cemetery had turned into a chicken coop because they dirty everything so much. I came to do some cleaning, but they did not appreciate the intrusion. When my husband and I came down to the crypt, they swooped down in a nosedive against us in order to stop us from descending."

"Like in Hitchcock's film?"

"Yes," she said unsmilingly, "like the film. They attacked us with such fury! Every time we had to carry sticks to defend ourselves."

We continued our descent and now the path full of hairpin turns skirted a rocky embankment, the amphitheater gradually became more and more narrow, like a funnel, as we went down, and the "garden" was replaced by tangled wild vegetation dominated by euphorbia with mastic trees, myrtle, and junipers growing among the rocks. At one point the path leveled off, widened, and came to an end at the foot of a great vertical dolomitic wall. There I saw the tomb. The bas-relief of the sarcophagus was almost the same pale rosy color as the wall, so that the figures appeared to be carved in the rock. A statuette of a guardian deity had been placed nearby. On the ground were other stones with inscriptions, some small saplings grew around, and nothing else. But that apparition of the figures in the rock, so unexpected, made a strong impression, as when all of a sudden the traces of an unknown civilization are revealed to an archaeologist and the wild and secluded place suddenly becomes full of mystery, because of these signs.

"My daughter, Elena, loved this house very much," the Signora said, using her daughter's name for the first time. "Often, she would come down here."

She spoke as if only to herself, in a soft voice, bent over the stone with her daughter's name—*Elena*—engraved upon it, as she arranged some flowers in a vase.

"And now I too come here often to visit her."

It was rapidly becoming dark and we climbed back up.

"My grandfather was a singular type," the Signora's husband said to me. We were seated outside, on the circular loggia with the columns I had seen from the sea so many times. "He collected antique arms, Oriental art objects, vases, porcelain. . . . Now there is nothing left. They carried everything away, even the furniture."

"I know that they were also at the Villa Bismarck. They must have come from the sea."

"They could also have come from Capri."

"Up until a few years ago, these things never happened on Capri."

"You can see that they are catching up. . . . I told you about my grandfather. He wanted to be embalmed. A doctor and friend did it, the one who embalmed the body of Pius XII, using the same ingredients. He had given precise instructions. Now he is laid in the crypt, lying on one side and with his head lifted up, toward the house, just as he had wished."

The Signora asked if I would like some tea. When she returned and offered me the cup it was already dark. Between the white columns of the terrace some stars shone in the still pale blue sky.

"The rocks are the true wonders of Capri, not the sea," she said. However much she forced herself to make conversation and be kind, her voice was distracted and disengaged, like a person who speaks and has her mind on something else.

"Until a short while ago, this was the most beautiful sea in the world," I said.

"Until a short while ago? It hasn't been that for over thirty years. . . . In this month once upon a time, down below at this hour, we would see so many lighted fishing boats, *lamparas*, that the sea was full of lights, they were like swarms of fireflies. Then all the fireflies went out. . . ."

She stopped for a moment, and then she continued. "But the rocks are always the same, they seem as if they had just cooled off."

". . . The construction of the geological landscape," I repeated from memory, "is so distant in time that if the wing of a flying reptile were etched in the sky, no one would have been amazed."

Finally, the Signora smiled, the shadow of a smile.

"You've been reading my *Guide to Capri* carefully," she said.

"I read it well because it was written well, as is obvious from the sentence I was quoting. Furthermore, it is not written in the neutral style of a Baedeker, nor does the style ever become affected as can happen when one speaks too much about the 'beauty of Capri.' Whoever speaks of the 'beauty of Capri' should be punished with a rap on the knuckles, or at least with a fine."

"Then me too!"

"But you make one feel the beauty, you never declare it

directly. I have never seen so much information condensed and so well organized in a guidebook. And then it reads—I was about to say—like a novel."

"One of those slightly boring novels that are being written nowadays?"

"But no, your *Guide* is never boring. It is a rational guide and it is made out of good reasonable prose."

"I worked so hard on it. It was my only refuge. Sometimes it was for me an exercise in survival, like the kind that the Marines undergo. . . . Anyway, it kept my head occupied. Most of all that chapter about geology. Geology is not my subject. I'm an archaeologist."

"I know very well. But to me your descriptions seem almost poetic in their exactness, even in their syntax. If a guide can resemble a literary work, yours succeeds without ever claiming to be one."

There was a pause of distraction in her, a brief embarrassing silence, and in order to overcome it, I said, "In your *Guide* this island appears not only beautiful, but disquieting as well."

"Disquieting in what sense?"

"I don't know. Look at the paintings of Diefenbach, for example. He saw it as disquieting."

"I never liked those paintings."

"Me neither. But you wrote in the *Guide* that Gustave Doré was inspired by these rocks for his illustrations of Dante's *Inferno*. What is more disquieting than that?"

"Is this a disquieting place to you too?" And she indicated with a sweeping gesture, the house, the rocks, and the entire landscape that could be seen from up there.

"I would say yes."

"I cannot manage to pull myself away from this place. Now I

can find my peace only here. Some discover it in looking out upon the agitated sea. . . . But let me tell you something that perhaps justifies what you say. . . ."

And she told me how one evening, upon entering the house with her daughter, she heard heavy breathing in the darkness of the room.

"Like that coming from the *Grotta delle Felci*?"

"No, no, it was different. It was not a natural event, it was as if a person were hiding behind the furniture. That was my impression, someone or something, very close by. I turned on the light but there was no one. However, that labored breathing continued. It lasted quite a while, and that was disquieting, truly disquieting, as you say."

"And how do you explain it?"

"I don't know. I can't explain it, even now. We couldn't find a trace of anything."

"It could have been a bird."

"Sure, a bird," she said thoughtfully, "a bird of evil omen. An owl, a barn owl. But the breathing was like that of a person, oppressed by an unspeakable anguish. Fear overtook us that night, both my daughter and me."

"And did it ever happen again?"

The Signora hesitated. "No. . . . Even though I often wake up in the night and it seems like it is always there, in my room. . . . Maybe it is just inside of me."

"But what is it?"

"That anguish, that breathlessness."

She then changed the subject, and at a certain point I asked her husband, who until that moment had listened to us without ever interrupting, I asked him if—nothing less—Newton's theory of universal gravitation was always valid, that is, constant, or was it also subject (how could I say this?) to that other equally universal law according to which everything decays and comes to an end.

He fixed me with his light eyes, immersed in quiet desperation, and smiled. "How come you ask me such a difficult question?"

"But you are a physicist, a famous one, right?"

I do not remember exactly how he answered me, but it seems to me that he said everything decays in time, that time is a human concept, and that we know nothing about an "objective" time, of a time outside time. Perhaps he wanted to play a joke on me because I had obliged him in spite of himself to enter into one of those astronomical conversations that sometimes are had on Capri, when one lingers on certain evenings, to take the fresh air on some terrace, to adapt to the almost always grand landscape and to a sky almost always overflowing with stars.

MY HOUSE UNDER
MONTE SOLARO

Whenever I come up here, to my little Capri home at the foot of Monte Solaro, I fear that I may have been a bit rash in buying the place at my age. To get here I have to walk up 150 solid, rustic steps, and for how much more time do you think you can manage that, a voice whispers softly to me. But when I finally arrive, it is as if my house wanted to reimburse me for the effort I have made and for the thoughts that have accompanied it. There is a terrace with two white columns floating in the sky, observing from on high the Faraglioni and the spacious expanse of the ocean on the horizon, where on the clearest days the Capo di Palinuro appears; behind me Monte Solaro rises up, like a rocky amphitheater, and occasionally, on clear mornings, I have seen wild goats standing still upon a rock peak, enjoying the first sunlight. And so when, coming from Rome, after two hours by train and another one by hydrofoil, I climb here, I feel as if I had suddenly flown through space and time into a world of water and rocks still at its beginning. Maybe it is because here nature assumes unusual and imposing forms, or because this house of mine is not far from the *Grotta delle Felci* where paleolithic beings once lived, who fished and swam in this sea, and who once climbed these millenary rocks, and saw the same landscape that I am looking at from here today. Surely the effect of displacement that is felt after a journey so brief and the encounter with a Nature so exorbitant is truly very powerful. However, there are also those hours when everything becomes gentler and acquires the lightness of a watercolor: the country-side of vines and olives, sloping with terraces down to the Marina Piccola, the soundings blue-green and blue in the trans-parent water around the Scoglio delle Sirene, the Sirens' Rock, and Capri, which from a distance appears like an Algerian vil-lage of white and rose-colored walls, and a stretch of the Sor-rentine Peninsula, faded by the sun to the color of wisteria.

It is no small thing to live the entire day face to face with all three hundred and sixty degrees of this panorama. It is neces-sary to be well trained and fortified in spirit to be able to bear it. But, if one can manage it, he can acquire at times the illusion of fitting like the right piece, even if cut imperfectly, into the great universal puzzle, and of perceiving something of the mysterious design that holds it all together. And standing before the perfect indifference of the morning sky, one can discover in tranquility the absolute equivalence of everything, while the noise of the coffee rising inside the coffeepot blends with the noise of an air-liner flying over the island.

In my house I can live for days and days as if it were a her-mitage, in perfect solitude, and even meditate upon the great themes that come to mind in contemplation of such a landscape. The racket of the life milling around in the piazza and in the streets pounded by the crowds of tourists does not reach here. Here time passes into a pure state and sometimes it seems measurable only by the monotonous nocturnal hoot of the horned owl. The mornings fly past burning my head, the afternoons are long and stretched out, and occasionally the night passes with its train of stars like the ocean liner Rex, punctuated with lights, in Fellini's *Amarcord*, carrying away with it the desire for a life that would never be and dreams that would never be realized.

My Caprese summer is composed of these things and of these moments, but not only of these alone. There is a rustic life that goes on all around my home, from May, when suddenly everything erupts into flower, until October, when clusters of small round grapes hang from the pergola above my table where we eat. And there are days when Vittorio, the farmer king on this land, seems transformed into a Vietnamese guerrilla with his tank of copper acetate, his mask and protective helmet; on other days, he shows up with an ancient present, a basket of figs. Up here there are geese, ducks, hens, whose fussing you can hear, and rabbits, goats, and even some pigs, raised by Vittorio with loving care before he makes a feast out of them. Evening comes with the smell of manure in the air, an ancient odor that seemed to have disappeared, pig manure, nourishing plants and helping them to grow. Vittorio is proud of that and abhors chemical fertilizers. But whenever I wander up here, through this tangled countryside, I try to avoid the borders of Vittorio's bestiary and his rabbits with their quivering little noses pressed up against the wire mesh of their pen. By now I have such pity for all animals and I feel so close to them that even a cockroach cannot leave me indifferent. If by chance upon my small piece of earth I find one upon its back, groping with its legs toward the far sky, I rush to turn it over, as if to correct a greater wrong done to every unacknowledged living species.

Vittorio is a hunter, but he doesn't brag about it with me because he knows that I disapprove of his passion: frankly, he cannot understand me. He knows and has tramped all the paths on this island that is so small but full of secret inaccessible places that only people like him know how to reach. They were accustomed to hunting quail that used to show up from Africa (those were the days!) and would rest among the rocks, halfway up, where there are no paths and where few *schioppaiuoli* (mighty hunters) were willing to take risks, having to clamber up the rocks or lower themselves into fearful crags with infinite drops and follow other routes unknown to anyone.

Vittorio talks about the quail with nostalgia, his mouth watering, because so few arrive here nowadays. The quail began to understand that Capri was not the most hospitable place to rest after their crossing; where before they used to come in thousands. . . . Vittorio is also a "miner"; that is, one whose job it was to blow up rock with carefully measured explosives, in order to obtain stone for building homes, cisterns, terrace walls. Now this occupation has also ended and he has become a small contractor. It is Vittorio who supervised the renovation work in this house of mine. It is no minor undertaking way up here, if you consider how each stone, each sack of cement, must be shouldered and carried up those 150 rugged steps! I have seen them, the carriers, working, bent and sweaty beneath their loads like Egyptian slaves in movies, being followed by the wary eye of Vittorio. In Capri, despite bans, building is always taking place at a constant rhythm, and so there is an entire population of workmen like these, who become adapted to the heaviest work. You are forced to think that, in spite of everything, this island society's composition is still archaic, similar to that of the ancient world. When I talk to one of these haulers it seems impossible to me that such gentle faces still exist, so humble and submissive. And I vainly look into their eyes for some flash, some sign to tell me where the virtual violence I observe behind their resignation keeps itself hidden, and I wonder if this is only a reflection of my guilty conscience.

The days pass the same up here, but on Saturdays and Sundays even here one feels something out of place, something disturbing the balance of the natural order of things. From Naples, from Salerno, from the port of the Marina Grande, the motorboats arrive in packs and they storm the island like the *pasdaran* on the attack from a ship in the Persian Gulf. They pass through the Faraglioni at top speed, smashing with their propellers the enameled blue sea and the sacred silence of the morning, and they drop their anchors next to the two or three most beautiful places on the island, at Cala Ventroso, the Grotta Verde, or the Cala del Rio, always calling to order there a floating condominial reunion. From the plastic cabin cruisers with kitchenettes floats the smell of charcoal, tables and dining areas are set, while mothers and their children soap up in the showers (because we have on board showers, but not water purifiers.)

On the weekends, it is best to avoid the waters near Capri; and even the piazza should be avoided, so invaded is it by the crowd of tourists and Neapolitan *pendolari*, day-trippers, who outnumber the local population by almost two to one.

Other days, I often go off in search of some place, a gorge, a rock, a cove, any place with a bit of clear water, where there are no bathers, unreachable by the drones of rubber boats, those pestilential mosquitoes now the masters of all our coasts. After I have managed to carve out a marine nook for myself, I lie down and immediately I feel "tough and elemental" like the island's white stones. I listen to their dry sounds as they roll, or I swim skimming a wine-colored stripe formed by the sea at the waterline around the rocks. Sometimes I lie upon my beach towel, enchanted, staring at the innumerable layers of that green glass, transparent upon the pebbles along the bottom, a few steps from the beach. How innocent and pure is that aquamarine, how virginal and precious in its delicate chromatic range! In contrast to the furious blue-green cobalt prevalent here, with its hard and almost impossible tones, this humble celestial note that delights the beach is so restful.

Under the water the sea is deserted of all life, only scanty *cefalotti*, little mullets, no longer than a finger, dart between the rocks busily seeking food, and the Mediterranean's own *saraghi*, thin as wafers, and shoals of anchovies that escaped being caught in the nets at sea. The marine bottom is always beautiful to look at. These depths are the most beautiful in the world, but it is as if an H-bomb exploded here, leaving things intact but killing all life-forms. I swim above these depths like an astronaut flying above an abandoned planet, gazing at lunar zones, Martian wastes, lichen vegetation out of sci-fi, all dominated by a silvery, purgatorial light. . . . The sea has been reduced to this. And here is a plastic dish and there a bottle, a can, a jar. . . .

On the night of the full moon, you go to The Grottelle, near the Arco Naturale, the Natural Arch, and dine outside before a Wagnerian scene, all rocks and precipices reaching out from above the sea. At other times you go to Augustus, to Tiberius, and rediscover the simple ambience of long ago Capri and a panorama that has remained intact. You see Capo di Minerva (La Punta della Campanella) and the Sirens' Islands (I Galli) and in the azure-rose ash of evening everything appears wrapped in myth. Or else you visit Paolino's at the Marina Grande, in a garden of yellow lemons hanging from the pergolas. And all around, in the air, in the people, there is something unreal, as if all those people seated at their tables didn't understand why they were together. Perhaps it is the unreality of our society surreptitiously revealing itself in this way.

My Caprese summer is composed of these habits and modest

recreations, but sometimes I must ask myself why my life up here is so often beset by an acute melancholy; why I must record with so much bitter pedantry every tiny detail that reflects the decay of things and people, and even weather; and why, even when the beauty of this island overtakes me, then most of all, I must feel inside me, like a torment, a sense of ending, a regret, a state I cannot define, that I call "Virgilian" and that prevents me from accepting all the beauty except as a mirage. It is my relation with nature that has changed: my feeling for nature is no longer what it used to be, no longer thoughtless, and here on Capri I am more aware of it than in any other place. It is a feeling born from a traumatic experience caused by my generation, and only by them, in the entire history of humanity. We alone have lived, in the brief span of a single lifetime, from a time when nature (sea, earth, sky) was the same as it ever was, to a time when it is no longer like that, but is sick, suffering, discouraged like the ocean floor. How, then, can we enjoy its beauty with a merry heart, how can we admire a panorama or beautiful scenery?

When the light of the sun sinking behind Monte Solaro illumines the Faraglioni hour after hour with different hues of yellow-gold and sulfur, amethyst and mother-of-pearl, rosy gray and lead, reflecting them in the still mirror of the sea, or when in the morning the beautiful day attempts to clear a path through the haze of the greenhouse effect, then I look at the world from up here and it seems to me that everything still might not be, and yet it is.

I feel this more here than I do elsewhere, in my country home near the sea, during these empty vacation days, while on the terrace I await the coming night.

ON A ROCK ONE MORNING

It was rather early. The sea of the Marina Piccola was without a ripple, blue and transparent in the morning peace. At that hour he was the only one who went down to the beach to bathe. Later, toward noon, the coming and going of the motorboats and the outboard motors and the rubber dinghies would begin, and the sharp odor of gasoline would be dispersed in the air. So he had two hours, three at most, to enjoy his rock in the solemn calm of Cala Ventroso. Once they were past the second rocky spur of the shore, the inlet appeared. "There it is over there," he said as he pointed it out to the boatman, a flat rock raised just above the surface of the water, isolated in the midst of the silent little cove, and all around there was a lovely aquamarine color owing to the shallow bottom of white pebbles. It was a comfortable place, dry and breezy, good for taking the sun.

He jumped onto the rock, taking with him his towel, rubber goggles, and a sack with his lunch of a peach and a *panino*. He told the boatman to return at a quarter to noon, and when he could hear that the boat with its outboard motor was far away, and silence was reestablished in the inlet, he was pleased to have had this idea. How beautiful and grand that point of the island was, and in the early morning how beautiful were those marine dolomites, tinted azure by the air, that fell straight down into the blue from a dizzying height. He felt like Robinson Crusoe, surrounded by pale blue on the virgin little island, and sighing with pleasure he stretched out on his towel. The sun was scalding, and his body absorbed it. He felt it enter his skin, pass through his flesh to the very bones. In a few hours he'd be as dark as a bedouin; he was of Mediterranean origin, so the sun baked him without burning him.

When he felt himself cooked to the proper degree, he dived into the water, and the contrast between the heat and the cold passed from his head to his feet like a beneficent current of energy reanimating him. He swam with long slow strokes; with patience he had acquired such harmony of movement that swimming didn't tire him, and swimming like that he could surrender to the joy of the water that ran along his body in an endless, repeated caress. He turned over in a dead man's float, and let himself be cradled for a moment. Now he saw the towering cliffs rearing straight up against the sky; a jet passed over, streaking the sky with a horizontal white plume, and space seemed immense. Then he returned to his rock to offer himself to the sun with renewed vigor.

That first moment, with his body still damp and cool, and the sun shining on his wet skin, his dripping hair drenched with coolness, was the best. All his pores opened, and he felt invaded by the smell of seaweed and rock, and a marvelous sleepiness took possession of him. He liked being just a body, concentrated and circumscribed in his physicality, feeling how exactly his body terminated in his arms and legs, fingers and toes, adhering like a limpet to the rock, all his corporeal being forming a single entity with it.

While he rested like that on his belly, with his face resting on his folded arms, he raised his eyes, eyelashes dripping water and salt, and he saw that a seagull was perched on his rock. The bird never moved as he watched it. His feathers were rumpled and disheveled. He was trembling and barely able to stand on his slender threadlike legs that stuck out like reeds from his downy belly and ended with three clawlike webbed toes in a raw pink color. Ignoring the man's presence, he poked with his beak among his feathers, and he was all feathers, a little heap of feathers in which the beak and sometimes the entire head disappeared. He must be terribly thin, he thought. Still poking with his beak, the seagull raised one wing, and he could see the skin was wrinkled and irritated in the angle where it joined his body. This detail too made him think he must be dangerously thin. Earlier, when he'd arrived, the boatman said, nodding at the seagulls that were circling around, "They must be starving—hear how they scream? They eat mice and lizards and whatever they can find, because there aren't any more fish in the sea. The trawlers stretch out their nets, and when they've passed by there's nothing left, nothing at all."

The seagull had stopped poking his feathers with his beak, and had assumed that position of absolute immobility that only birds have. He stared at the sea without caring about it.

At this point he remembered that he had a roll with salami in his lunch sack. Who knows? Maybe he'll like it, he thought. Cautiously he moved one arm, to not frighten him, picked up the sack, opened it, and tossed out a slice of salami. The seagull suddenly turned toward him, but he didn't fly away. He stood there, still immobile. And while they remained here, face to face, he and the seagull, it seemed to him that the slight distance that separated them was in reality more insurmountable than an abyss, and that nothing, no pity, no gesture, would ever be able to bridge it.

Once again the seagull's immobility was shaken by a feverish shiver that climbed up his legs and seemed to reverberate in each feather, almost causing him to lose his balance. Was he sick? The difference between him and me, he thought, is that he, like every animal, expects nothing, and is never touched by the idea that his misery could be acknowledged. And all of a sudden he understood that the tragic dignity that he seemed to see in that gaunt, bald bird was at least equal to his own encounters with the indifference of the universe, and that the concentric and indecipherable eyeball of the bird, fixed on a sea devoid of fish, was the only possible response to that indifference.

The seagull shook his wings and flew away. His glance followed him and he saw in the circle of his gaze the steep rocks falling headlong into the sea, the pine trees clinging to the precipice, great erratic masses tumbling into the indigo water. He saw the sun glancing implacably on every stone, saw all that energy blocked by the immobile misery of things, and saw in nature the same tragic dignity that struck him in the seagull. Can it be that all of nature is suffering? he asked himself. Am I just getting old, or has something really changed? Still, within this same nature, I'm fine, I swim the way I always did, with the same agility, and I enjoy the sun and the coolness of the sea with the same pleasure.

He was disappointed with himself, with these thoughts of his. It seemed more proper not to disturb the felicity of the beautiful day with his inclination to philosophize, and above all he didn't want to leave the state of pure physicality in which he was indulging. He stood up to dive in again, but suddenly he discerned with indignation that the water around his rock was not as clean as before. A current had arrived carrying on its surface white foam, plastic bags, a watermelon rind, a cardboard box, a scrap of newspaper, refuse floating on the pretty pale-blue transparency around the rock. He saw that the powerboats were already arriving off shore, and he understood that his moment was almost over.

Realizing the short time remaining, he dived in and swam toward a point where the current of dirty water didn't pass. It made him angry that a place so beautiful was ruined, but by now the whole of Italy is falling in ruins, as if it were inhabited by monkeys, and what do monkeys know about beauty? He reached the stretch of clean water and touched the bottom with his foot. He stayed like that, as in a *bain marie*, half in, half out of the water, for a while. He recalled that many years ago— thirty, thirty-five?—he had come to the same place, on those same rocks, on that very rock, and he remembered the water, its pure brightness, and the unsullied sea, and he remembered going swimming with his beloved friends, he remembered their names echoing in the air, their young faces and their happiness, and he heard again their shouts and laughter, their exclamations at the magic of that sea. Wasn't it here that Ilaria had stepped on a sea urchin? Trustingly she had put herself in his hands, stretching out on the rock so that he could pull out the spines one by one. Sometimes a love affair began like that.

All at once he was struck, not so much by the nostalgia for the voices of that nature and that time, but by the absolute certainty that it was all over. Then he thought that even the sea urchins had almost disappeared. So much talk, he thought, for Pasolini's fireflies, and are the sea urchins any less poetic? They sparkled like splinters of glass, blue, violet, lilac, or copper, topaz, rust. You had to be careful where you put your feet, and how good they were to eat! They were the caviar of our youth, the one luxury we could allow ourselves. That's over too, and the hermit crabs with their contorted shells, and the sharp-edged black mussels, and the little crabs and the sea fleas, and the starfish, and even the limpets have become rare. And the colors, and the thousand transparencies of Capri, what will become of them? he asked himself. Now there are just these ugly squat plastic powerboats, the stink of gasoline, the noise.

He returned to his flat breezy rock, no longer happy as before, even if the sun blazed down and the streak of filth was far away, and everything around him shone. He stretched out, a pleasant somnolence descended upon him, and he fell asleep.

He slept deeply, who knows for how long. Then he heard some hushed youthful voices very close by, and thought he was dreaming. When he finally woke up completely he rediscovered himself on the rock, and saw three small boys who were fussing with a net, a bucket, and other equipment for fishing. He began to listen to what they were saying; he always enjoyed listening to what children say when they're sure no one is listening.

"You'll end up in the pot tonight, pal, that'll teach you to escape."

"What is it?"

"*Un pint' 'e rré*. Look what beautiful colors!"

"It's a *marvizzo*."

"It's a *pint' 'e rré*. A *marvizzo* is green all over."

"Let's put it on the hook as bait."

"What for?"

"Let me have it and I'll show you."

"I won't give it to you if you won't tell me."

"Give it here. Don't be a dope. He's got a fishing pole with a long line."

"What do I care?"

"Come on, give it to me, I'll show you how to fish with a fine seagull on the line. I already did it once."

"Come on, give it to him, it'll be fun."

"Then we'll make him fly at the end of the line, with the hook and the fish in his belly, like he was a kite."

"Yes, yes, look, there's one!"

"Then you'll give it to me?"

He intervened. "Don't do that," he said.

For a moment the boys went silent. They didn't expect a grownup to intrude in their game. Perhaps they hadn't even noticed him, so absorbed were they in their fishing. Then one of the three got up the courage to ask him, "Why shouldn't he do it?"

"You can't figure it out for yourself?"

"No."

"Because with that hook in his body the seagull would suffer and die in a horrible way. Didn't you think of that?"

"No."

"Well, use your imagination. Imagine how you would feel with a fishhook in your body and some kids having fun by yanking on it."

"But I'm not a seagull," one protested. The other two laughed heartily at that response. Encouraged by his unexpected success, he began to play the clown.

"I'm not even a fish."

"Not even a *marvizzo*."

"Not even a crayfish."

"Not even an octopus." At each new example the other two laughed.

Then he heard the chugging of a motor. It was the boat and the boatman who had come to pick him up right on time.

CAPRI AND NO LONGER CAPRI

And so I'm here on Capri and no-longer-Capri; the continual malaise that grips me comes from the sensation that everything is no-longer, and is more lost with every passing day, inexorably. A vacation is the best time to give oneself over to awareness of this fact, because on vacation all our time is at our disposal to contemplate the vacancy of everything, no daily business distracts us from observing the world, and everything in the universe going downhill. And when from my terrace I look at the line of the horizon, I seem to find myself in a kind of outpost near that no-man's-land beyond which everything becomes lost in nothing. In the city one isn't so close to the silence of the sky teeming with stars. One isn't apt to see the moon in the city, the glare of the sea at noon. One isn't in continuous contact with nature and its vicissitudes. One lives more unconsciously, and takes decay more lightly. It seems to belong to the city, to be a consequence of the city, with the city's concentration of men and machines. While in these lovely vacation spots where nothing distracts one it's impossible to take a vacation from the thought that everything is swiftly, inescapably, going to ruin. Here more than in the city one becomes sensitive to every attempt to alter the state of things that are altered daily with impunity. Here it becomes instinctive to become more concerned, for one notices the degradation more. But it is precisely this sharpening of instinct and perception that makes one incline to pessimism and disenchantment. No, says a voice, nothing will ever be restored to rights, everything will continue to go downhill, because there's a conspiracy of forces much greater than our awareness of the ruin. Because nature here is bound closely to beauty one is more aware of fragility, and one feels that the center of the misery is no longer in man and in history, but has been transferred to nature.

And so if in this clear September I see between two white columns the infinite calm of the sea and the immobility of the rocks mirrored there, my gaze is full of this disenchantment, and continuous interferences come between what I see and the illusion that originates in it. And this lovely island becomes the place where the gaze is exhausted.

Here on this island whose name is inscribed in my own, there formed the myth that I lived unconsciously in my youth. Here was formed the myth of *la bella giornata* (the perfect day) and of *dolce spensieratezza* (sweet unthinking), the myth of nature inhabited by gods whose voices were like our cries at midday. Here where we deceived ourselves into believing we were "the absolute masters of light," I have returned after thirty years, full of the awareness I've acquired, and in the interval, in these thirty years of absence, everything was used up and every god died. The place I had left was no more, my return was no longer possible. And this place in which I now find myself is a place that I do not recognize.

"While conscious, I want to be you, I want to possess your happy unconsciousness" (F. Pessoa, *Una sola moltitudine*, vol. 1, Milan: Adelphi, 1979). I owe my return here to this—this absurd dream. I dreamed the white column silhouetted against a bright-blue sky, the indolent vine clinging to it, the curved pattern of the blue and yellow ceramics, the fig split open in the warmth of the fields, the prickly pear with the sea before it, the taste of a lemon ice (what more could I ask for?)—all this I dreamed. And I thought that in some moment of perfection, in an ordinary day fallen from heaven like a benediction, that I could be that, my happy unconscious youth, yet remain conscious as I am today that my end is not so far away.

If only a little more than thirty years—about half my lifetime—was needed to create this mess that has turned my places upside down, wouldn't it take the same amount of time to reestablish the lost order? Well, yes, that would be lovely. But the path to disorder is infinitely faster than that toward order. Just one gesture can create enormous disorder, but how many gestures are needed to put everything back in order? Still, at least for now, I console myself, the world has gone on, in spite of the second law of thermodynamics, and in spite of the death that awaits it at the finish line, still the world has gone on, as I was saying, from the disorder of chaos to the order of universal gravitation, from the cacophony of imploded stars and earthquakes to the music of the spheres, the very music that in Kubrick's film *2001: A Space Odyssey* accompanies the voyage of the spaceship. And see how man is inserted into this universal machinery, like a grain of sand that could jam it up . . . and so these thoughts come and go at random like the clouds in the sky.

My terrace is gifted with such an excessive panorama and can embrace such a boundless expanse of sea and sky that one's thoughts are inevitably influenced by it. In fact, there's a vague and erratic mode of thinking I've experienced here that I call "terrace thoughts" for just that reason. They're thoughts that, perhaps out of a need to live up to the grandeur of the scenery, tend to lift themselves higher and higher, where the clouds come and go in the celestial realms, and, like the clouds, are committed to the eternal play of transformation and abstraction. Now the clouds condense until they seem to acquire solidity, and now they rapidly dissolve. . . . What a continuous theater of the ephemeral is performed right here! And how similar this representation is to . . . what? Better to interrupt at once the rush of comparisons, metaphors, symbols, analogies. Doesn't the rush of the clouds suffice? Usually at this hour they have an appointment on the crest of Monte Solaro, which looms behind my shoulders and provides the backdrop to this house with its steep walls the color of cardboard. There on the jagged rim of Solaro the fleet of the sky throws down its anchors with its white sails filled with the wind, and pauses for a moment before beginning its journey toward Capo Palinuro, invisible on the distant line of the horizon. *Accidenti*, damn, they've fallen again! The fleet, the sails . . . metaphors are seductive, they attach themselves to words even when the words are tired of putting up with them, above all when one is talking about clouds that now look like this and now like that, as we know, and from dawn to sunset combine all the colors. Thoughts, on the other hand, follow words without effort, they pursue them distractedly and dissolve with them. I'm speaking of terrace thoughts, which are always concerned with the largest systems because, as I said, they fly higher, they're "cosmic," eternal, sometimes even Leopardian, and they worry about things like order and disorder in the universe, and similar trifles.

All you need is to make yourself comfortable in your lounge chair, look at the clouds, and then these thoughts come of their own accord, so much so that you think, Hey, look at what I'm thinking! But what is it exactly that I'm thinking?

Looking at this starry sky from the terrace, I think about the grand cycles of the universe and, philosophizing in the style of the wandering shepherd of Asia, I say to myself, Why do those stars shine so brightly up there? Who keeps them suspended in the void? Why do the constellations not change, so that I can see them just as Homer saw them? And why do the seasons revolve and never err, and day follows night, the season of fallen leaves follows that of the flowers, and so on according to a preestablished order that sometimes has the beauty of a mathematical equation, or a well-shaped thought, or a verse that comes out right? And why was everything mixed up in the primal chaos, and water was confused with fire, the earth with the sky, and every element with some other? Why was there this inexorable and musical procession toward that order that still resounds today? Isn't it perhaps possible that, just as there was that progression from disorder to order, now there's a reverse movement, and everything is beginning to regress from order and beauty toward disorder and ugliness? I know, these are thoughts founded on air, but I'm also thinking them because, before I got here to this terrace with its view of the Faraglioni, like Dante, I passed through the streets and lanes of a grieving city, I saw its eternal pain, its lost people, and all the stars and my cosmogony together cannot manage to make me forget it.

It takes a certain heroism to live here. You have to conquer this house with hard work every day. One hundred and fifty steps, and every time you make it up to here you're bathed in sweat and out of breath. But all this suits me. A more comfortable house, reached more easily, is the life of a rich person here, and I wouldn't know how to live in the shoes of someone rich. I want just this house, hard to get to, and I want to earn with my sweat the privilege of having it. I like its simplicity, its few bare whitewashed rooms, the air on a veranda open to the sea, its peasant origins. I like the fact that it is constructed with stones carved from the living rock and put in place by the art of dry masonry. I like the fact that it's isolated in the middle of this piece of countryside at the foot of Monte Solaro, between the grapevines and the olive trees laid out in descending terraces. I like that it seems suspended in air, hanging between the sloping walls of the mountain and the boundless sea.

When I'm on the terrace I can see on one side, foreshortened, a bit of the Gulf of Naples, starting from Castellamare to the foot of Vesuvius, as far as Massa Lubrense. From the other side I can see the open sea past the Faraglioni and, when it's clear, far off on the horizon the coast of Palinuro. That village down there is the center of Capri with its white houses, in that kind of saddle where the island narrows between two gulfs. With binoculars I can read the time on the campanile in the piazzetta, see the awnings of Caffè Vuotto and Bar Tiberius, and the columns next to the funicular. This landscape, dominated by the geographical formation of the island, isn't the usual postcard view, for it is harsh and craggy, with the rugged lines of a scene by Hackert. In spite of this, I often feel a certain saturation, a kind of exhaustion from the landscape, and within me is born the desire for a more anonymous space, like that of a desert, without recognizable contours and without memories. Even if one pays no attention, even if one doesn't turn one's gaze deliberately, one is captured by this landscape, made its prisoner, and like a prisoner I sometimes dream about other, freer spaces.

I felt this landscape 'nausea' even when I visited the lovely exhibition of Neapolitan landscape painting held in the Castel Sant' Elmo in Naples. As I moved from one room to another and my eyes rested now on a gouache, now on an immense scenic view by Joli, I strangely reexperienced the condition of being a prisoner, a prisoner of history, of a place, or of a myth, and every painting was like a cell bar in that great conceptual prison that is Naples, with its past, its faded beauties, its songs . . . yes, the songs too, every song a prison bar. Beyond those landscapes, those scenic views, the myth, the history, beauty, and songs, was that open space where I longed to land, beyond that reality reduced to a perennial, compulsory, self-representation. In short, I believe there also exist "intermittences" in the landscape, spatial gaps, and here in this house on this terrace I sense them, sometimes perhaps in an exaggerated way.

I have become attentive to the smallest natural event, and if I note here or there some sign of decay, I at once become melancholy. So if from up here I see a streak of dirt on the sea, if I see too many motorboats invading it, if I find a tree with shriveled leaves, if an oak sickens and is cut down, if a grapevine is threatened by mildew, and so on and on, all these signals affect me, make me uncomfortable, apprehensive; such events disturb my peace or reduce me to such a state of acute sensitivity that when I see a tree I feel such intense pity for it that I want to embrace it like a person, or I am moved when punctually every morning a new hibiscus blossom, red and triumphant, comes out to replace the one just fallen off. Perhaps this state of heightened sensitivity is not just cultural—how to put this?—for Vittorio too, the farmer-owner of the fields around my house, manifested it spontaneously with no less feeling.

Since Vittorio died, life up here hasn't been like it was before; it's as if a presence were missing, a spirit of the place, that held together the plants, animals, and earth in a whole that is fragmented without him. One becomes aware of all this on incomprehensible evidence. Like everyone who lives on the earth,

Vittorio did nothing but complain about the weather and the seasons, about fruit that didn't ripen as it once did, about the interrupted cycle of ancestral modes of doing things, about pesticides that poison people and plants, and so on. And this evil that he saw diffused everywhere and spoke of as a hidden enemy perhaps was also a presentiment of the evil that attacked him from within, of which he was still ignorant.

I don't believe that the millenarian feeling of the end of the world, having emerged today at every level, is born in me simply from the fact that I'm approaching the end with rapid steps, considering the swift passage of time. It's also born from the accelerated deterioration of things and history in this second half of the century, and more particularly, when I'm here, from the proximity of my unhappy Naples to this house in which I find refuge and seek repose. This is enough to make me feel that I am not allowed an idyll when I am so near tragedy. And if I let myself be overtaken by this state of mind, sky and earth become gray and soiled like a crumpled old blanket, and the Faraglioni turn into two misshapen old boots tossed down there, just like Van Gogh's. And some evenings, when I am present for the melodramatic spectacle of sunset, a sense of absurdity assails me and I ask myself very seriously, What am I doing here?

And so it seems to me that Nature can no longer be the mirror of the soul, as the "extremist Romantics" believed, nor does it imply a connection to landscape. We cannot mirror ourselves in any landscape; no landscape is a reflection of our state of mind. Landscape just stands there in simplicity, mute; it doesn't talk with us, it is what it is, and that is enough. "Don't deceive yourself about places. All places are hard and earthly." Only the recognition that this is how things stand speaks to us. So even if there is natural beauty here, it is no longer possible to enjoy it. It is always accompanied by this ambivalence: there is natural beauty here, it's true, it still exists, it is here that one encounters it, but one no longer wants it or believes in it. Or perhaps one does want it, wants to be enchanted, but is too skeptical regarding it. And it's the same thing, I say this out of experience, with *star bene*, being well, enjoying life or vacations, and so on. This too is something one no longer wants. Willingly one would make do with less.

I hear the cry of the seagulls, those hoarse cries, ancient and mysterious, like the lamentations of Diomedes. A few days ago I heard those same cries in Rome. A colony of seagulls took up residence in the center of the city. Driven there by hunger, by the poverty of the sea, they were roosting on the cupola of the Church of the Gesù a few steps from my house. At night they drop screaming onto the nearby streets to feast on mice, refuse, scraps of food. Their cries are the cries of the starving, cries of street-cleaner seagulls, and in those nocturnal cries there's something tragic and degraded. So now when I hear the seagulls screaming here among the rocks of Capri their cry no longer comes, as it once did, from the sea foam, a messenger of freedom and space and wind. Superimposed on theirs is that other cry, that of the city seagulls, that disenchants and disheartens this cry, and unites with it in decay.

The consciousness of decay modifies our perceptions. A rubber dinghy pounding over the water with the noise of its outboard motor is also a part of this experience, and that noise can destroy in one stroke the enchantment of a silent morning. In an isolated haven, the simple apparition of a motorboat, with the consistency of plastic, is not merely a false note—it is a disturbing one from a metaphysical point of view. And if at one time a bottle left on the beach was just a bottle, now it's something indecent, like excrement. So at one time a smear of tar was just a smear of tar, and an abandoned tin can was just a tin can. Not anymore, not today; today they are signs announcing a catastrophe.

Aesthetic perception is also modified by decay, and when in one of the devastated cities of the south, after proceeding down roads and alleys full of garbage and desolation, you at last reach the church or monument you wished to see, how can its beauty be admired by eyes that images of misery and neglect still darken? What is attractive is infected by the ugliness surrounding it, and even if there is beauty there, a kind of infelicity is interposed between it and the visitor's gaze.

Perhaps this particular kind of wretchedness is now general and encompasses the beauty of this island threatened on every side; perhaps it is a sentiment new to the world and to our country above all, a form of impoverishment that no earlier generation ever experienced.

Everyone has—or, better, used to have—his own place, a landscape he bore within him like an image impressed in a memory deeper than any recollection. And when he needs a truce with life, it is here, to this place, that he dreams of returning. This place is as precise as a photograph, and its every last detail, down to the most insignificant, takes on value and an unmistakable meaning: a certain undulation of a hill, a tree standing on a precipice, a group of houses with their white reflections on the harbor, a rock or a pinnacle overlooking the sea, a meadow or an inlet. We insistently seize this or that detail, for it seems to us that all the particulars, that hill, those houses, that tree or rock, are a secure point of reference, the center of the world. We imagine they are immutable, there forever, waiting for us. But what happens? What has happened in so few years? The hill has been leveled, the tree cut down, the group of houses has grown gracelessly, the rock is covered with sand, there's an antenna on the rock peak, and a hotel disfigures the inlet. The places dear to us that seemed immutable are turned upside down, troubled, shattered, or totally wiped from the face of the earth. Their immutability is no longer a guarantee of our identity; no comfort can be derived from them any longer.

I ruminated on these thoughts one day, as I drove slowly and laboriously along the tortuous, fantastic road that follows the Costa Amalfitana. I knew the whole coast from Amalfi to Positano to Nerano, knew each succeeding inlet, and I'd explored the whole of it above and under water. Yes, those were the outlines of the landscape, and those were the cliffs, peaks, rocks engulfed in blue. It was all there in front of me; the color of the sea viewed from above was still a china blue, hard, compact, glistening, and with each curve in the road one still enjoyed the same vertiginous change of scene. But where was the magic? It was as if the landscape were ill, as if a pestilence had attacked and disfigured it. It was a slow and detailed destruction, stubborn, continually wounding the eye and the soul, that provoked this disenchantment. It was as if an army of parasites had taken possession of a beautiful leafy plant, devouring the roots, hollowing out the stem and branches, leaving only the outer covering. Nothing had been respected, no memory remained intact. And it seemed to me not only that places had been devastated but that I myself had been intimately devastated, and that an essential part of me had been mutilated. I was extraneous, and now I was again traveling through places dear to me, but I didn't belong to them and they were no longer a part of me, they no longer spoke to me; they came to meet me downhearted and altered, deprived of all their power to enchant.

As in a dreary game of three-card monte, a contractor with a long nail on his little finger, a mediocre, servile land surveyor, and Caliban, a buyer newly arrived, raise high ugly walls around the *bel paese*, the lovely country. . . . As Cavafy writes:

> *With no consideration, no pity, no shame,*
> . . . .
> *When they were building the walls, how could I not have noticed!*
> *But I never heard the builders, not a sound.*
> *Imperceptibly, they have closed me off from the outside world.*
> "Walls," *Collected Poems*

And what else has happened in these few years? Haven't we all been shut out from our world, from the places dear to us without noticing it?

When I went to Capri as a boy I didn't even have the money to pay for a hotel, because in my family we were not permitted to spend money for this kind of amusement. So I had to make do, and I stayed with two or three friends in one room in the Pensione Maresca, on the Marina Grande, renowned for its low rates. In the evening we disguised ourselves as viveurs, in colored shirts with ascots, but we couldn't afford even to sit down in one of the cafés in the piazza where the spectacle of Caprese life flowed like a glittering river. Our only entertainment was to look on, seated on the steps of the church; we were extras, *viveurs* transformed into voyeurs. At the center of the stage were Dado Ruspoli and Rudy Crespi with their exclusive clans and their court. What refinement! What whimsy! What elegance! Their movements, whatever their purpose, were spied upon from our gallery, speculated about and commented on. What can the immortals have thought up to amuse themselves more than we amused ourselves last night? Who will be included among the fortunate few? Where will the slender feet in their light gilded sandals carry them? Where will they go to have dinner, to chat, to dance, to snort cocaine, to be fashionable? Around the two young gentlemen crowded cheerful groups of ubiquitous cosmopolitans: a certain momentary celebrity, young wives in lamé with their escorts, dark figures with their shadowed eyelids and lips like silent-film stars', the billionaire of the day, a cover girl with her Latin lover, and so on. The former dancer Hans Spiegel, like one of the seven dwarfs, now old but always wearing a red hooded cape, Oriental-style flowing pants, and a cascade of Balinese necklaces around his neck, surveyed the piazzetta with pipe in mouth, to assure himself that life went on in spite of everything. These were the final years of the empire at the end of its decadence. Rudy and Dado were gorgeous, and even in their voices you heard the tinkling of money. Dado was more striking, not so much because of the raven on his shoulder but because of his natural grace, his extreme nonchalance. How I envied him that naturalness of a favorite son, with a life in which everything was permitted because he could permit it for himself! I was still so awkward, even in my glances and facial expressions, and how liberated Dado was in his dress, as well as in his lifestyle, without having the air of a dandy. He invented a new style every evening. One night he arrived with trousers like tights that even covered his feet, like a figure by Pisanello, and another evening he was dressed like a toreador with a golden waistcoat. One saw him and thought of the splendor of youth that nevertheless is fleeting, of the quick speech of a Mercutio, of his intemperate companions, of happiness that comes to him who desires it, and so on. Rudy instead shone better when to his beauty was added the perfect and somewhat repetitive beauty of Consuelo, his young American wife, as charming as the tiny bride on a wedding cake. When they appeared in the piazza together, smiling, with the whole world at their feet, they became the beautiful and the damned, or, rather, the beautiful and wellborn characters in a Fitzgerald novel, my "cult writer" of the moment.

Of that time I remember only dazzling images, stylized and mythicized by my imagination; after all, I was an inexperienced young man, under fire for the first time, as they say—and then I remember my parallel life on Capri, made of penury and deprivation that I hardly noticed, not giving it any weight, so engrossed was I in marveling at everything that was happening around me, and if by chance I met a girl who liked me, I almost always lacked even the possibility of inviting her to dinner. I had to avoid her during the hours in which one goes to restaurants, and make a date with her for the beach. At that time the sole consolation, the only real lover who gave herself freely and with abandon, was the nature of this island, her small pebbly white beaches reached by canoe, her sunny rocks and enchanted transparent waters. There, in her scalding womb, in some grotto, cave, or gorge, summer loves were consummated.

Today that Capri is no more, but now that particular Capri doesn't matter to me so much. Everything that evokes the myth of Capri, the life of Capri, her characters and their madness, the name of Capri itself pronounced with inflected emphasis by the Capri specialists, now merely provokes in me a kind of disgust. The most illustrious representatives of that Caprese life, with their dreams of the Mediterranean sun and their mania for earthly happiness, all those types who, as Cerio wrote, "never did anything extraordinary, but certainly not ordinary either," those famous "beautiful people" so often sung about, those profligates, aesthetes, mythomaniacs, nuts, who lived here bewildered by their false images of themselves, and who believed themselves to be at the center of the world just because they found themselves on this island—the lot of them, to tell the truth, are today, seen from a distance, a little pathetic. And no less picturesque than the fisherman Spadaro, or the tarantella. Even Lenin, in the photograph where he's playing cards, with Gorky, sometimes has the same effect on me.

The dirty water that on some days arrives from the gulf, clouding the transparency of this sea, bears a fatal message. It says that the forces of evil that have overwhelmed my beautiful city and have disfigured it irreparably, forever, are advancing in closed ranks upon this island to lay siege to it and reduce it to the same humiliation. And in truth it isn't the dirty water alone that carries this message. On a Sunday in August, it's enough to go to the piazza to observe the faces of the people who've just come off the ferries and are sitting down for a coffee. Looking at them, how can one not despair? Ugly mugs, bruised, sad shapes, gallows faces, post-gallows faces, faces "full of will and empty of meaning," all good manners, all restraint lost. For many years now this piazza has not been a center of cosmopolitan worldliness but an observation post where it is possible to analyze in a tiny space, as on a laboratory slide, the degeneration of the society of the south in its rapid, inexorable transformation from a civil into a criminal society.

Vincenzo, the waiter in Bar Tiberio, tells me that Bacon—Do you know him? The famous English painter? Of course you do, the one who paints faces like gobbets of meat from a butcher shop, yes, indeed, Bacon—has come to sit here many times. Vincenzo even asked him for his autograph. Oh yes? He must have come here for inspiration. Where else would he find faces like these?

Faces of hyenas, morays, lions, lemurs, iguanas, gorillas,

beech martens, tranquilly pass back and forth, like the faces in the film *Star Wars,* as if there were nothing amiss.

Sometimes one has a sensation that the enormous wave of tenements that has submerged the towns of Portici, Torre Annunziata, and Castellamare, as the lava of Vesuvius once did Pompei and Herculaneum, is continuously advancing, spreading uninterruptedly, as far south as Sorrento, coming from the immense degraded metropolis to pound violently on this island in order to overwhelm it. Note well: corruption in construction and in the environment always advance in step with social corruption. What new San Gennaro will come to stop this lava flow?

Clear water, even more than blue sky, is among the essential elements that come together to determine that disposition of the soul, that feeling for the world, that I call *la bella giornata,* "the perfect day." When I arrive on Capri, I almost always find myself in the heart of my perfect day, for where else are the waters of the sea as bright as on Capri? Where are they so crystalline and transparent? There are other places surrounded by a pure and luminous sea, Sardinia for example, and the Aeolian Isles, Corsica, but it is difficult to find concentrated in such a brief stretch of coast such a prodigious and contrasting range of colors, filtered by that very special light reflected by the rocks and depths here.

Whoever immerses himself in these surprising waters asks himself by what mysterious alchemy is there an emerald green here while only a meter in that direction the water becomes like a sky of Dante's "Oriental sapphire." What sorcery changes the quality of the water and its transparency from one point to another with such precious color combinations? To swim in Capri's water is to feel yourself invaded by the azure-green–deep blue in its infinite gradations. It means to feel yourself resounding inside like a musical scale, with the same impalpable lightness, the same elusive sensations that music provides. *This* is what the water of Capri is like, or, rather, was like. Underwater were seen glassy reflections that seemed created with the special effects of crossed searchlights, while above, on the surface, all was at perfect pitch, the gong of the sun blinding at midday, the howl of blue, the scream of green, the explosion of high-intensity azure. Have we truly lived in that world of untenable light? Haven't thousands of years gone by since then? Does it take so little to ruin everything?

A tiny beach with white pebbles is hidden between the clear pale-blue depths and the rocks bordered by subtle submarine transparency. The sea rolls the pebbles, and the pebbles give off the sharp rattling sound of chopped ice. It's the only noise emitted by the gentle rhythm of the waves, glassy at its source. Every pebble is smooth as an egg, hard and compact, buffed perfection with nothing left over. Finding words like these pebbles, precise and complete in themselves, made only to say what they say, inventing a way of arranging them that is as fortuitous and harmonious as the beauty of this beach: this was my first guide to aesthetics, acquired here.

The sun blazes ideograms of light, with incandescent Oriental writing it inscribes every wave. Nuclei of more intense light explode radiating in the air, break into flakes under water, rhomboids, trapezoids, lozenges; they weave trembling geometries of light outshining light. The decomposition of light enlarges the field of perception like a magnifying glass. Music of transparencies, one inside another like Chinese boxes, as blue enters gentle azure and vanishes in the absence of color, diminishing by infinitesimal gradations as far as the line where the sea meets the sand. And how every pebble is transformed and chimes when the water merges with the sun and floods it with liquid crystal!

I dive in and pass through the strata of the many-colored transparencies, I confuse the musical sequences of greens with blues; as I swim I return light to light, mobile grids of gold threads flash with lightning, a net woven of rapid blinding signs envelops me. It flashes in my wake, beneath the foam of my feet kicking the crawl, "the numberless smile of the sea." This was a morning on Capri forty years ago.

Perhaps it may seem exaggerated, but today every time I go to the sea to bathe I experience yet again Adam and Eve's expulsion from paradise; I don't know how to define otherwise what I feel. At one time swimming underwater was an approaching adventure; there was a sea heavily populated with fish that would come up close to see the object in my hands shining in the rays of the sun. Grasping the aluminum gun like a thunderbolt, I took aim and pierced them as they swam, with the serene indifference of a god who doesn't know what pain is. Then the time of innocence ended and the inhabitants of the sea knew that it was better to stay far away from man, and even the newborns that had never seen a gun fled, driven mad by its glittering. By now the survivors were few. The sea was no longer the aquarium of God; it was no longer an oceanic El Dorado, and from that dazzling gun and that ungainly creature who grasped it came only extermination and death. Over and gone was the time of lobsters caught barehanded and that of the *saraghi* and *orate* that moved tranquilly among the rocks, and to transfix them was not an impiety then. The sea became in a few years a Dead Sea, fish were only seen frozen on the fishmonger's counter, as at a morgue, and the nets became ever more close-meshed.

All the fish disappeared, and not even one remained alive to swim in the waters of the sea. No, there did remain one, a *cefalo,* a gray mullet, which had become lost and stopped one day before the point of my gun. He looked at me, we looked at each other, both surprised. He was tiny and weak opposite me, but he didn't run away. I aimed at him. A voice said, Shoot, go ahead, shoot, finish your fine project, and I lowered the gun. All my gear, mask, fins, knife, suddenly seemed out of proportion, ridiculous. I was ashamed of that empty sea, and for an instant I felt myself on the other side, on the side of that solitary little mullet, at the mercy of everything and everybody, like every threatened living creature.

Ah, the time when the Gulf of Naples was my Polynesia, and every rock my coral reef, every beach my atoll, every landing that of Captain Cook! The time when I went hunting *spigole* like Captain Ahab, and harpooned one as big as Moby Dick. The time when I swam the crawl like Johnny Weissmuller and approached every girl with the inexperience of Tarzan with Jane.

Certainly everyone's youth is far away for someone recalling it when he is older, but our youth is farther away than that of any other generation, because for us everything has changed in the most rapid and disturbing way, and everything has become unrecognizable: cities, places, rocks, islands, earth, sea, the seasons, the scent of an orange.

There is more myth and history in a small wave of the Mediterranean than in all the water of all the oceans mixed together, someone wrote. It's true; the equatorial seas are richer in fish, forms, colors. Yet here when I look at the beautiful depths of pale rock under water, the sea meadows with rising and falling ribbons of Poseidonian algae sparkling in the diamond transparency of Tyrrhenian light, blocks of stone, solitary and grand like sculptures by Moore, I feel myself penetrated by the grandiose stylistic coherence of this sea. It's a Greek sea in a conceptual sense too, an idea that rises up in the mind. And I can do no less than think that if the Greeks fought and won at Thermopylae, it was because the well-defined contour of a column, a statue, or a temple could be sharply profiled, like these submerged rocks, in the unchanging azure of the Mediterranean; it was because they had defeated every Asiatic, overfull, Oriental, and boundless proliferation of forms. The essential beauty of this sea is repeated in each of its elements, in every pebble and grain of sand, in every drawing-near of colors and transparencies, in every silvery and textured fish scale, in every shape of fish, and in the elegance of its emblem the dolphin. Fishes tattooed like forest savages don't rise from these depths; among the chinoiserie of coral reefs one doesn't see a Kandinsky-fish, a Klee-fish, a Picasso-fish, or a Miró-fish, and so on, in a crazy carnival of submarine disguises. In this sea one doesn't see anything that is too gaudy with frills or surface squiggles, but only severe lines, sober and pure, and colors of a chastity and a Morandian rigor, or of an absolute intensity without escape. In short, this is the image that our sea offers of itself. And when my friend Claudio Magris sends me a postcard from the Scilly Islands in the Atlantic, asserting that the ocean embroiders around these islands transparencies no less refined than those seen here, I respond with another postcard: But tell me, can you dive into that ocean, or does its intense cold reject you? Can you lose yourself in it in a warm embrace while you're swimming the crawl? Can you mate with its welcoming waters? Because even the temperature of this sea of ours is that of a great loving body to which it is sweet to entrust yourself.

I will always remember the day on which, from the altitude of five thousand meters on the Milan-Palermo flight, in the extraordinary morning transparency, I saw in one glance the

Circean and Pontine islands, Ischia, Vesuvius, Capri, as far south as Palinuro, as far as the tall majestic remote mountains of Calabria, all together in the circle of one glance. So portentous was the vision of that land of gulfs and volcanoes beneath me, so azure the Tyrrhenian in which it was mirrored, that it seemed a dream. And I too thought about the Immortals, who "as if lying in deep marriage beds, leave behind sacred imprints of their bodies, eternal traces of primal beauty." Who if not D'Annunzio could express it with such words? But immediately afterward I imagined those same places seen not from an altitude of five thousand meters but from close up. And a sad lament like a *melopea*, a dirge, rose from my heart. This sea is lost, I thought, and all the bays, beaches, laughing seascapes of the Italian coast, for more than six thousand kilometers. Lost are Miseno, Cumae, and Baia, the Phlegraean Fields exhaling sulfurous vapors; lost are Lucrino and Trentaremi and Nisida with their beautiful names. Lost the gulf of the Siren Parthenope, of Lucullus' and Statius' poetry, lost from the cape of Posillipo as far as the shores of Vesuvius, more lost than Pompei and Herculaneum, from Portici to Oplonti, Vico Equense and Seiano. Lost to us is the Sorrentine Peninsula dear to Minerva, with its hanging gardens of lemons, lost the transparent water of Nerano, Amalfi, and Positano, of Licosa and Palinuro. Lost is Paestum, and lost, so very lost, Calabria, from one seacoast to the other. Lost, alas, lost is Sicily where the waves still have the color of wine, lost the city of temples and the prison caves of Syracuse where stupid measured barbarity is revealed, lost solitary Selinunte and Segesta, and Noto and Catania, the Conca d'Oro and sweet Palermo. Lost, lost, forever lost.

I beg pardon, but I don't experience nostalgia, regret, disenchantment as elegiac feelings, but as nonresignation. I can never resign myself to this loss that dishonors a generation, and was so tranquilly accepted by everyone. The real earthquake down here was not the one that destroyed houses by the hundreds but that which built them by the thousands, and one never saw more wretched or pretentious prisons. Easy money made scorched earth all around. Not much was needed to make money—an extortion, a drug shipment, a kidnapping—but to spend it well culture is needed. The old culture was dead, the new not yet born. They spent their money very badly; they dirtied and disfigured everything. The one who could have stopped them didn't do it; he was in Rome, busy with the game of *correnti*, of trends and bank accounts, and with the Cold War, unaware that the real war was this one that was destroying the *bel paese*. There was no parliamentary investigation of beauty and ugliness; no one ever made it the focus of a national referendum. Indifferent to the unique patrimony that history entrusted to them, the senators never exercised their right of veto in the name of the Italian people. They preferred the pardon: Catholic, apostolic, Roman.

My élegy is inconsolable, and deeply felt, not in the least romantic. It is born of the sadness that emanates from these places that still cling to the illusion that they are places but are mistaken, for in reality they are non-places. Is Taormina now a place, or merely a name? Someone traveling in Italy now meets only names that belonged to very beautiful places, meets spectral non-places, devastated ex-places, unnatural pseudo-places. Someone coming to Siren Land finds the Waste Land, the land of the Sirens transformed into a desolated land. So-called culture, that which counts, never ceases to be up-to-date, and never loses the opportunity to say how things used to be done; but it always speaks of things already completed. It never reacts, never really rebels. Has anyone, just one person, because of grief or as a protest, ever been seen to give himself to the flames in the city square like a Buddhist monk? A loss so enormous would merit it.

"It is as if the entire social form were to fall to pieces and the human element were to swarm in the disintegration, like worms in cheese. Streets and railways are built, caves and mines opened, but the whole organism of life, the social organism, is slowly crumbling and emptying itself out in a kind of process of dry putrefaction, very terrifying to see. Thus it is as if we found ourselves at the end with a great system of streets and railways and industries; and then in a world of complete chaos, in turmoil above these constructions as if we had erected a scaffolding of steel and yet the whole body of society was going to pieces and putrefying within. It's a very terrifying thing to understand; and I have always experienced this terror on a new autostrada in Italy—more than in any other place" (D. H. Lawrence, *Etruscan Places*, 1932). Prophetic Lawrence!

Once there was Goethe's *Italian Journey*, and that of Stendhal, and Madame de Staël. Then there were the Italian journeys of Gissing, Douglas, Lawrence. Today there are the journeys of Ceronetti, Vertone, Celati. A bit of comparative literature in school wouldn't do any harm.

There are days in which the sad procession of refuse passes slowly and touches everything, heedless of this or that place, and passes over everything with the cruel obtuse indifference of a natural calamity. The current arrives from Salerno and from the Gulf of Naples, from the coasts of Lazio and those of Campania, where waste can be discharged and is transformed into frothy foam, bubbles, and slime, or into the filthy soup of floating garbage. But worst of all is the deceptive detergent, spreading over the surface of the sea that continues to deceive us with its transparency, covering everything with an impalpable, invisible film. If you barely stir it with an oar, bubbles emerge. One bubble is enough, just one of these bubbles, to put me in a bad mood, to ruin my perfect day. How many stories lie behind one bubble! But that malignant bubble announces a new form of suffering, a kind of depression, a psycho-ecological stress that now strikes everyone.

Where once there was the sea of the gods there will be a huge sewer; rats will bathe and swim in that sewer, and they'll even say, This is great! because if for a rat all the world is a sewer, even the sewer will have its natural beauties, its landscapes and its sunsets. Those rats will be trained and satisfied rats, rats in love with their sewer and incapable of thinking of a world other than the sewer. They're certainly not going to come to blows, like me, for a detergent bubble floating on the water.

What was the world we loved? It was that world of colors and transparencies of which Pissarro, Manet, Monet, with their luminous sunbathed paintings in the open air, of which Renoir, Degas, or Matisse, looking out from the balconies of their rooms, seem to have wanted to leave the final and marvelous image, to make us feel more deeply the pain of having lost it.

The world we loved was that sea battered by shining liquid gems, that palette vibrating with living colors to be applied unsparingly, those blues veined in green, the restless roses and azures, the pale sky blues becoming visible, the enameled cobalts, the dense intarsias of lapis lazuli, the elaborate arabesque transparencies. What we loved were the days in which all the colors of the island were set aflame, as in a Fauvist canvas, with its colors laid down by the brush or the palette knife in one stroke, one essential blob, absolute, chosen by exclusion, and charged with all the power and bursting force of elementary signs.

At present, we know, Beauty exists only to be profaned. So it is for the Blue Grotto, so it is for every opening, grotto, or

sounding of this island, continuously visited, explored, ran-
sacked, and suffused with gasoline and its fumes from boats and
scows loaded with tourists and bathers. They insinuate themselves under the natural arch of the Green Grotto, disturbing its
precious emerald waters, into the entrails of the Red Grotto
edged in indigo, and everywhere it is possible to make merchan-
dise of and mortify the lovely body of Capri. The intrusions of
these boats into every most secluded recess or exiguity of the
coast evokes the humiliation of the physical the new army
recruit undergoes, anal inspection included, with the gloved finger of the doctor deeply and painfully exploring that place. This
sodomizing, this total and demoralizing *grottazzurrificazione*,
"Blue Grotto-izing," of Capri is truly unbearable, as it was
found to be "unbearable" by Andre Gide, when he came to the
island at the invitation of D'Annunzio. Henry James, seeing the
rowboats that entered the tiny opening of the Blue Grotto,
imagined "how delightful it would be" if a wave were to block
the entrance and the boats, with their cargo of tourists, were to
disappear inside forever. At heart I understand him. I too, when
I see all those boats entering, prying, photographing every possible opening of the coastline, think "how delightful it would
be" if they were to disappear, swallowed up by an avenging
spirit of the place. As may happen to the rest of Capri.

It is useless to dream of the old rowboat, the silent poetic little boat that allowed only those who earned it with the healthy
work of rowing to reach the most beautiful and immaculate
locations. Now any place is reachable without effort by any
motorized slob.

The cabin cruisers arrive, especially in the high season; they
come in swarms and throw themselves, roaring, spraying foam,
farting, into the few harbors of the island, filling them with
crowds. They're ugly, noisy, stinking, not made for sailing, and

on the sea they're out of place, resembling bathtubs, bidets, gross latrines with cabins that gargle with the power of a hundred horses behind them. Strutting, arrogant, pretentious, with prows that seem shaped by a hatchet, ridiculous pyramidal bridges and sharpened noses that lack the graceful crescent of a true bow but possess the stupid pointed shape of a goliard's cap, these gadgets of the Sunday coasting trade are distinguished only by their oversize engines. The more powerful the engine, the more powerful the owner thinks he is. Rather, one might say that the sole reason these contraptions have been built is not so much to navigate as to demonstrate in action the potency of the owner. Who are these owners? Ah, to hell with them. They rush about inside their gigantic polyester hulls, ridiculously aerodynamic, deafening, spewing gasoline, roaring, farting around the island. They invade the most enchanting coves, eat, shit, jettison the leftovers from their lunch and all the plastic containers they brought with them; they throw away bottles and tins that end up on the bottom, and they take off in a cloud of fumes.

Sometimes I dream of being the emperor Tiberius. In my dream I order all the owners of these cabin cruisers to be brought into my presence. I have one smeared with fuel oil; another I have buried in garbage, another is forced to drink a full liter of gasoline, still another is condemned to die slowly suffocated in a plastic bag, and so on, always applying the Dantean principle of punishment as *contrapasso*. And then I have them all tossed from the Leap of Tiberius, precipitated headlong into the crystalline waters of Capri that, finally vindicated, await them down below, clear and laughing.

These days the devil "loves the sea," and brings his family to the sea for a snack. For his feast the traitor chooses the most hidden corners, the most secret little grottoes, the most immaculate little natural swimming pools; he lands on the most fabled rocks and on the most untouched beaches of the island, and where he has landed all magic is at an end, because the devil has a full meal, with first course, second course, and dessert, and leaves the remnants wherever he pleases, and doesn't give a second thought to smashing beer bottles on the pebbles, scattering in them the seeds of sharp splinters.

Some Sundays I see Capri from up here like her poor little blue lizard, covered with an army of black insects that are devouring its dead body. Or like a bone—because Capri has the shape of a bone, narrow in the middle and flaring at both ends—like a bone we throw to dogs. Or it's like an ant, minuscule in comparison with the huge crumb of tourists that it must drag away. Or finally, like a pearl or a daisy, and so on and on.

Still, it's strange that the jurisdiction protecting marine parks does not extend to Capri. What must have been the bureaucratic considerations that determined the exclusion? If there isn't an *alga*, a seaweed, or a tiny fish to save, wouldn't the blue lizard have sufficed? And that miraculous combination of water, light, and rock that on Capri produces such extraordinary colors and transparencies, is that any less precious than a seaweed or a tiny fish?

> *Here, on the level sand,*
> *Between the sea and land,*
> *What shall I build or write*
> *Against the fall of night?*
>
> A. E. Housman

At a certain hour in the afternoon, very early, between three and four o'clock, the sun hides itself behind Solaro, "great regulator and dike of the sunlight," and shade covers this house on the slope of the mountain. This shadow is still clear and transparent, like that of an awning on a beach, pleasant because it alleviates the heat of the day, and it moves gradually toward the Faraglioni until the sun is no longer hidden and evening falls.

So from four o'clock on, the house is in the shade and consequently I look out upon a landscape the sun illuminates until late evening. The effect is theatrical, like gazing from the darkened orchestra at a stage lit by spotlights. I'm fine outdoors in this shade, looking at the island shining before me, with its gilded rocks against the azure. The shade is restful, and that light down there does not hurt the eyes; they can contemplate things calmly, from a distance. While things change color and alter, I am here with a book or a newspaper in my hands, but I can do no less than think about how I too with my years have entered the zone of shadow. And from this shadow, still transparent, I look at the world and life and the day that passes so fair, trembling and full of ardor, like a marvelous spectacle.

That line of shade cast by Solaro dividing Capri into two zones makes me think of other shadow lines that we must cross, as one crosses a mysterious threshold beyond which we know not what to expect. And my thoughts come round to the feeling that overtakes us, to that hesitation, that doubt, before we cross it. Everyone has his shadow line to get over, but we all have a definitive and final one. Is there another life beyond that line? The question is, shall we say, rather embarrassing. I put it to myself often, particularly here, while I'm on vacation. But there is something reassuring in the absolute peace of this day that dies without a breath of wind, "in the certainty of the resurrection."

Sometimes when I think about my death, I think more about how life will be without me than how it will be in a beyond about which it is perhaps useless to speculate. And how life will be without me I already know: it will be perfectly the same, and perfect days will continue to shine on the sea, and the light will vary from rose to violet on the Faraglioni at sunset, and everything will be as it is now, as it is in this moment. And I may now also pretend that I am gone, and look at everything as if I were not here. See, I'm doing so; I look. The sea is flat and calm and seems to become one with the sky, there's a kind of felicity in the air, and nothing, no thing or creature in the whole universe, seems aware of my absence. Eternity must be like this. All of a sudden everything seems to tremble as if it were painted on a paper backdrop—Time has returned—and when everything reforms and recovers its customary aspect, I discover myself here contemplating the "usual deception" from my little Tibet on Capri in the somewhat rarefied air of the evening.

I had a dream. The face of my watch filled up with water. The hands came loose and floated in that water. No more hours may be measured.

It seems to me there is no doubt about its meaning.

This dream, however, has made me think of that other shadow line that we all cross every night, to speak with that other I that is within us, or to be spoken to by it. "Yes, I'm asleep, but at the same time powerful dreams keep me awake," wrote Kafka. It happens to me too; but my unconscious must not be endowed with much imagination, for I almost always have the same dreams, recurring dreams.

I dream of being an actor in a play. The show has begun. Around me all those onstage are reciting their parts; it will be my turn in a bit, and I don't know who I am, I don't remember anything anymore, neither the character I am supposed to represent nor the quips I'm supposed to speak. I don't even know the plot of the play, whether it makes people laugh or cry, anything. And now the moment for me to speak has arrived, the public is there waiting, the spotlights are on me. What will I say? The dream goes on within this anxiety.

I dream of having to take an exam, but it seems to me I have already passed it, and anyway I haven't studied, I'm not prepared. What shall I do? Am I going to show up or not show up? But I can't not show up, it's an important exam, a decisive one. Do I show up all the same, even if I don't know anything? No, I won't go, I already have my degree. But when did I take my degree? I don't recall very well, perhaps I am mistaken, I'm really afraid that's how it is. Will I be called, will I be questioned, what will I say to the examiners, unprepared as I feel I am? This dream too is prolonged in anxiety. . . .

I dream that once, a long time ago, I committed a serious crime. It seems, but I'm not sure, that I killed someone. This fact has just come out quite unexpectedly, because I had forgotten it completely, and even now I don't remember anything, I know only that this crime occurred, and that the police, on the basis of what clues no one knows, have taken up the investigation that was abandoned years ago. Will it end up with me? Will they arrest me? I will pay for that crime that I don't even remember. And why should they remember something that I have forgotten? So much time has gone by, can it be true that I committed that crime? Isn't time enough to cancel it? Perhaps it is all a dream, yes, I'm dreaming, it's a nightmare that keeps me in a state of anxiety, that I created by myself, and that I myself by rationalizing a little can make disappear. But the dream continues, the police investigate, I'm frightened, the crime is serious, perhaps it really took place, and useless, useless is my claim of having forgotten it, of believing that it never was. . . .

I dream I am in a foreign country and I don't have the money to pay for a return ticket. I spent everything I had with me without noticing, perhaps because my figures were wrong, perhaps because I was improvident. The ticket is very expensive, yet I *must* leave, I absolutely have to leave on tonight's flight, otherwise I don't know what will become of me. I can't stay here, that much is certain. Will I find someone at the airport who can lend me the money, a friend, a fellow citizen, an acquaintance, whom I can repay as soon as I get home? And so, puzzling over these various possibilities, on a deserted Sunday I hang about the desolate streets of a decaying metropolis, full of insecurity, of apprehension, of anxiety, while the hours pass, and it grows late, always later and later. . . .

Without granting them too much importance, as an exercise or an exorcism I've explained these dreams to myself like this: In the first, which takes place in the theater, anxiety is manifested in the emptiness of a world where one no longer recognizes the meaning or knows the part he's supposed to play. In the second, that of the exam, is manifest the anxiety of someone who doesn't feel he has fulfilled himself but believes it is too late to try again. In the third, that of the crime, is manifest the anxiety of having denied or annihilated a part of himself at the dawn of his conscious life, a part that might have lived and whose presence in some way he still notices. In the fourth, that of the foreign country, is manifest the anxiety of not being able to turn back, of being too distanced from one's true being to be able to ever go back.

In each of these recurring dreams—which repeat themselves with assorted variations—there is at bottom a forgetfulness, a distraction, an omission. As if I had committed a grave fault against myself and had not lived the life that I should have, which I have inadvertently let escape. But one could say the same thing of every one of us, I expect, and therefore I ask myself if the analysis I've made of these dreams is correct, and if it is not, I prefer anyway not to expose it to the scrutiny of psychoanalysis. Better to leave the sediment at the bottom of the glass, if it's there. Why remove it? To muddy all the water? At least this way one part, the most revealing, remains clear. And after all I am not unhappy at my removal; I believe it stimulates creativity. And my innate agreement with the world, and my ready disposition to grasp felicity when it is offered to me, are the Trojan Horse that I've introduced into the enemy city, the city of shadow, and that I, like every Mediterranean, believe comes from the light, and I must then be an expert, in my own way, about light and shadow.

Yes, my life, like that of every man, is begun in disorder (and what else is death?). But it has meaning when it opposes itself—in vain—to this destiny. If I think again about the broken mosaic of my days, I see that not even today, with the wisdom of then, would I be capable of rearranging the little pieces in one way or another to form some kind of understandable pattern. Therefore there remains always in me that desire so well expressed in Omar's quatrain:

> *My Love, we might conspire against Fate*
> *To change the sad manuscript of life!*
> *Would not we tear it into a thousand pieces*
> *To recreate it nearer to our hearts' desire?*

"Casually the days go by / and indifferently the nights," I too would like to begin, as Blok does in his "Violet of Night." And I would like to write of these days and these nights. To annotate life as it comes, as it comes now, in this moment in which nothing happens. To take a sample of water from a river or a sea, to analyze it with the only means I have, this heartbeat, this absentmindedness alert to background noise, a distant noise, with a little note played softly that always announces the end. To take a small portion of my vacation time and by means of this sampling to make it catch a glimpse of that larger time that includes it, of my way of perceiving it, or of the fundamental unease that passes through these my wandering hours. To let oneself go, to speak, in the writing that comes exactly as the time of which I am speaking comes, to gather up not the immediacy but the duration that is the breathing of things, a breathing that I observe better from my observation post up here.

A vacation, leisure—as I read in a small book by Starobinski—may give life to a literature of the day and of the comparison of various types of days. To reach the naked essence of this idea, and from this terrace that seems a raft between sky and earth, without "the hindrance of one who submits to the rules of urban duty," to relate the use that I make of the days, and recover their possession.

Such might be the Horatian "cultured leisure." But too often it seems even to me that this is impossible in the present time. Neither the "open spaces of Nature" nor "the modest enclosure of a country house" can any longer provide the hoped-for relief. It is impossible for the sea to "abandon itself to the felicity of the beginning," impossible "to live withdrawn outside the tumult," impossible to distance oneself from the "corrupt city."

However, there is here an hour, the hour which for centuries was dedicated to meditation and to prayer, that instead happens to be dedicated in an extremely hazy and almost narcotic way to the mystery of life. I've said this with almost the same words as my friend Parise who loved this island and knew it well.

For me this hour that arrives like the call to prayer of a muezzin, this hour of recalling, is the hour when the whole house and the countryside around it after the long ceremony of sunset, are wrapped in a profound silence, scarcely broken by the distant cough of a motorized fishing boat, which cuts the surface of the calm, flat sea of mother-of-pearl, and by the rustle of water in a pipe. Ilaria is watering the plants. She has a colored kerchief on her head, a sari draped around her body, bare feet. I look at her sideways from my lounge chair while I pretend to read the newspaper, admiring her beauty, and melancholy that no trace will remain of this lovely image I have caught of her.

(But actually there may be a trace; it's a figure painted by Piero in Arezzo, and Ilaria comes from there, from Arezzo, so there's nothing strange in my associating her now with that figure. While she waters the plants, thoughtful, I see in her neck the same columnal grace, with her head gently poised above it like a capital.)

Sometimes I seem to hear time pass concretely, with an audible swishing sound like that of a jet of water gushing from a pipe, or like that of my inner ear, the obstinate buzz that has accompanied me for years, which is heard more loudly in silence, in the drawing near of evening, with rising humidity.

The black cat, a Persian with long fur, is poised next to a gecko. She stares fixedly at a point on the wall for hours, unmoving in her Asiatic impenetrability. The other cat, the one with tiger stripes and a white muzzle and face, jumps up on my lap and searches briefly for the most comfortable position for herself, as if I were her pillow or her favorite couch. So as not to disturb her I avoid even the slightest movement. Finally she finds the right position, folds her feet under herself, and assumes the form of a floating gosling. After a little she closes her eyes and purrs; she's already gone into a trance. Her inert little paw is soft as a tiny sponge; I press it lightly between my fingers.

The dog stays farther away on the edge of the terrace. He seems absorbed in the contemplation of the landscape, his gaze is a bit unfocused, and his wolf's muzzle is tensed to take in the smells and noises, imperceptible to me, coming to him from the countryside. Profiled against the blue of the evening and resembling his progenitor the divine Anubis, he adds something to the sacredness of the hour. He has the outline of a jackal, the pricked-up ears of a dingo, and the hieratic pose of the dogs of the pharaohs. But his eyes, when they rest on me, are the affectionate ones of a mutt. He thinks he's a puppy, even if he is three years old. He's a spoiled baby of a dog, I often say to Ilaria, you see it in his behavior around other dogs, always breathless and eager to participate in any kind of excursion, like Pinocchio when he followed the bad boys. Then he turns his head toward me, with his two dingo ears upraised like fingers in a V for Victory sign.

I had the roof whitewashed, had some help with the walls of the rooms, and had the shutters painted. I've had two cypresses planted, an arbutus, and many other plants. I had a cement basin constructed, four by four meters, which we pompously call the "swimming pool." You bathe in this tub, you're refreshed, and you avoid going down to the sea when you don't feel like it or when it's too crowded. Is it thus that my love for the sea will end? A distressing end. It seems that on the island the applications for swimming pools have increased, and are directly proportional to the impracticality of the sea. On Capri, of all places!

In today's *Corriere* Vertone warns us, "Basically in our luxury yachts almost all of us have comfortable cabins, and we enjoy furnishing them with care, never concerning ourselves with the holes in the hull. We Italians are the hull, for we are cunning, and we aren't interested. It's everybody's problem, so nobody's. If piling up treasure in the cabins of a ship is the same as accumulating wealth for the fishes, that fact should be understood, and it takes imagination. And cunning people don't have it, they haven't time to imagine the future."

Capri is my luxury yacht; on the other hand, seen from up here, it really seems a ship, and this ship too is beginning to spring leaks everywhere. Here too on Capri everyone improves his cabin to make it more comfortable, and I'm no exception. Here too we are cunning, and here too, above all, some imagination is needed to imagine the future.

I came to Capri during this February of 1990 that seems so much like spring. The weather is marvelous, and you can sit out on the terrace to take the sun. The newspapers say this is the mildest winter anyone can recall. In Florence it registers twenty-three degrees Celsius, in Rome twenty, in Palermo twenty-four. I quote from the article I'm reading: "A warm shudder runs across the land, and experts talk about the greenhouse effect, but one of these experts notes that we lack scientific evidence to prove it. It seems that only in 1782 was there such a temperature in midwinter, which makes it two centuries since it has been so warm, to the point where February turns into May. But if it happened two centuries ago this means that no greenhouse effect is involved and that Nature is unpredictable. The optimists say this. Others instead say that in 2030 in Rome they'll be cultivating date palms. Still others say that one can know nothing because in this field it's hard to forecast even tomorrow's weather. At any rate, the Earth is warming—on this there are no doubts—but we don't have a reliable scientific interpretation of the phenomenon."

And this fake summer dominates all Europe. In Italy (naturally) there's "an anomalous assault on the beaches" and many bathers, profiting from the unexpected and somewhat suspect heat, have come to Capri to go bathing. From up here I see two people swimming in front of the Sirens' Rock near the Marina

Piccola. . . . How beautifully the mimosa has flowered! I've never seen it so yellow! And the peach trees extend their already pink branches against the blue. Even the other plants have bloomed early. It's a disturbing springtime, and it almost seems that it isn't April but February that is "the cruelest month."

"But if it's fine to take the sun in February," says the newspaper, just what I'm doing now, "perhaps it will be less fine this summer to turn on empty water faucets. Drought lies in ambush and allergies too, it seems. Those who study the psyche speak of the destabilizing effects of an early spring: apprehension, headache, anxiety."

POSTSCRIPT

Capri and No Longer Capri is a book by chance, and this for me is its limitation and perhaps its merit, if there is any. It is a book that was born of a commission, profiting from some pieces published here and there in different times and circumstances, but which directed my hand as I was rewriting and completing them. I tried to give the pieces a sense of wholeness, utilizing and integrating strategically those already written with new ones, in order to lead all of them to the final outcome and to capture its center, as in a game of chess.

I had in mind, also from a literary point of view, a Capri inserted into a larger Mediterranean context, and so I sought a style to replicate those books written by the travelers of the Grand Tour, still filled with the wonder of discovery, in which the immediacy of the impression was suddenly set down upon the page. And the names Goethe, Gregorovius, and Douglas do not appear by chance in the first part. But I am also reminded of other, nearer Mediterranean writers, such as Lawrence, Durrell,

Cavafy, and the early Camus of *L'Eté* and his descriptions of Oran; and then of Montale, of Quasimodo, and even the Penna of *"Il mare è tutto azzurro / Il mare è tutto calmo. / Nell'aria è quasi un urlo / di gioia. E tutto è calmo."*

The word *Mediterranean* almost implies the word *decadent*, because it signifies the history of the encounter between romantic culture and its myth. And a little decadence, like the predilection for beauty, perhaps suits me, and has informed naturally my style of writing, but without making it—at least I hope so—aestheticizing.

But the real occasion for this book is born also from the fact that, after a thirty-year absence, in 1982 I returned to Capri, and returning there where I had been young—especially in a time of rapid and visible changes like ours—can be a disconcerting experience. And so was my experience, because the change was not revealed to me immediately but little by little. I noticed it within myself like the feeling of an irreparable loss that I met again in things and in people, in the nature and the beauty of the landscape seen from the terrace of my house.

"From this place a landscape painter could easily draw two tall rocks of marvelous shapes that are on the coast: they are called Faraglioni, and they number among the small extraordinary features of the globe." So it is written in an old guidebook printed in Naples in 1826. I would have liked to be that landscape painter, I would have liked to name as he did the Faraglioni for the first time, to be able to feel in such a manner. Instead, standing before those "small extraordinary features of the globe" I felt a melancholy that I could not repress, and it was this feeling of loss about which I have written.

This island "whose name is inscribed in my own," forms a part of my "personal geography," and I have written this book in order to give an account of my presence here as well, in order to speak of the spirit of the place and of that which "dictates within," and perhaps for me too to enter into that secluded *cimetière marin* of literature dedicated to Capri, and in consideration of its students who do not easily forget who has passed through these parts and has left his testimony.

With a method much like that adopted for *L'armonia perduta*, I have recounted my relationship with this island in an indirectly autobiographical, narrative-essay form, followed by a personal journal of superimposed and contrasting states of mind in which I seek to express the contradiction that is in the book's title by means of variations in style; that is, the simultaneity of two contrary sensations, because the relationship between myself and nature in these places is always so pronounced (as in *Ferito a morte* and in *L'armonia perduta*, that relationship between my city and myself). Sometimes I sought refuge in narrative pure and simple, and sometimes in my "reflections from the terrace" that always derive from the fact that I am on Capri, and from the fact that on Capri, as in all the loveliest places on earth, one can always discern best the impending threat of that finality, of the "world's disorder" that inevitably makes us consider decadence and the end of all things. I always tried not to enter directly into the ecological argument but to keep my distance, fundamentally, and it has taken much effort, literary effort as well, to avoid that language: for example, the word *decay* I tried in every way to replace with another, but I had to use it all the same, unwillingly sometimes, when it was unavoidable.

I do not wish this book to be read with a feeling of nostalgia for what Capri once was and is no longer; just as I did not want *L'armonia perduta* to be read as an elegy for good times past. It is desire and not nostalgia that better explains how we are what we are, and how things have reached the point they have. And the desire to reencounter those places where our roots reach down also matters, in order to—even through writing—reappropriate them and "make them feel at home in the world."

My return to the island coincided with my sixtieth year, a private "shadow line," slightly different from the one in Conrad's story, but no less meaningful; luckily, this "still clear, transparent" shadow, has also entered my book. Just as that sudden spring had broken its agreement with time, an anomalous spring appears on the last page and arrives in February, February 1990: everywhere the sun is shining, the air is warm, the sky is blue like enamel; but it is winter—we cannot forget it—and there is a certain anguish in the air. . . .

R.L.C.